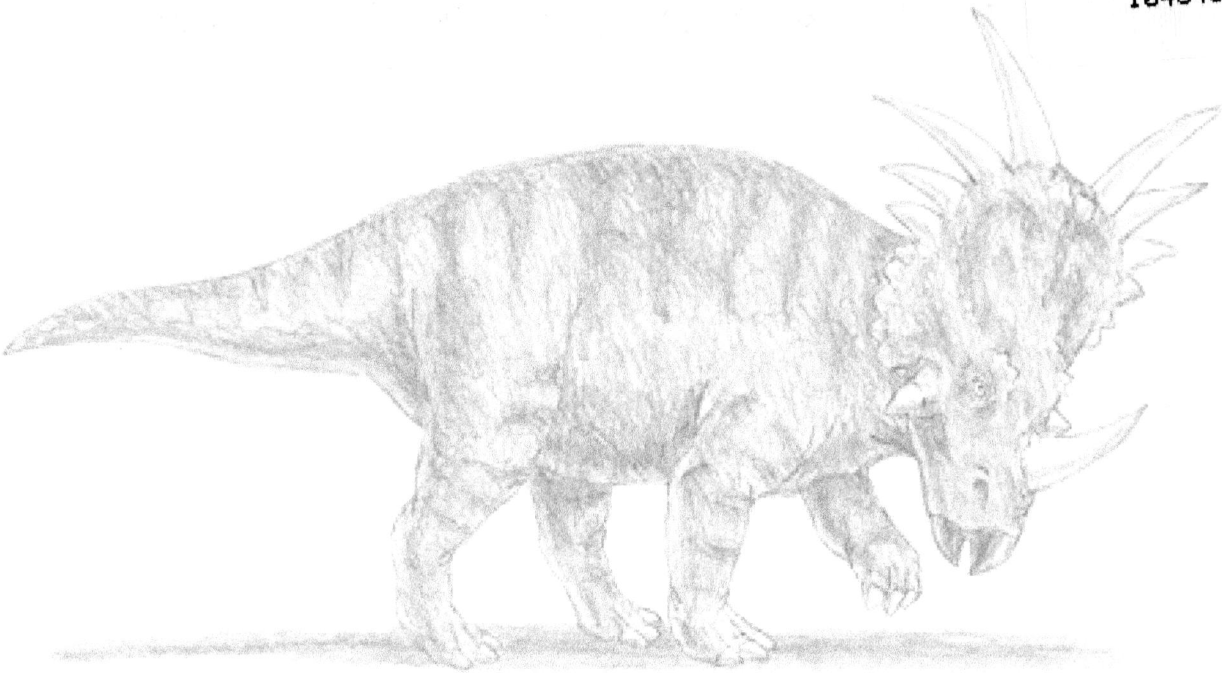

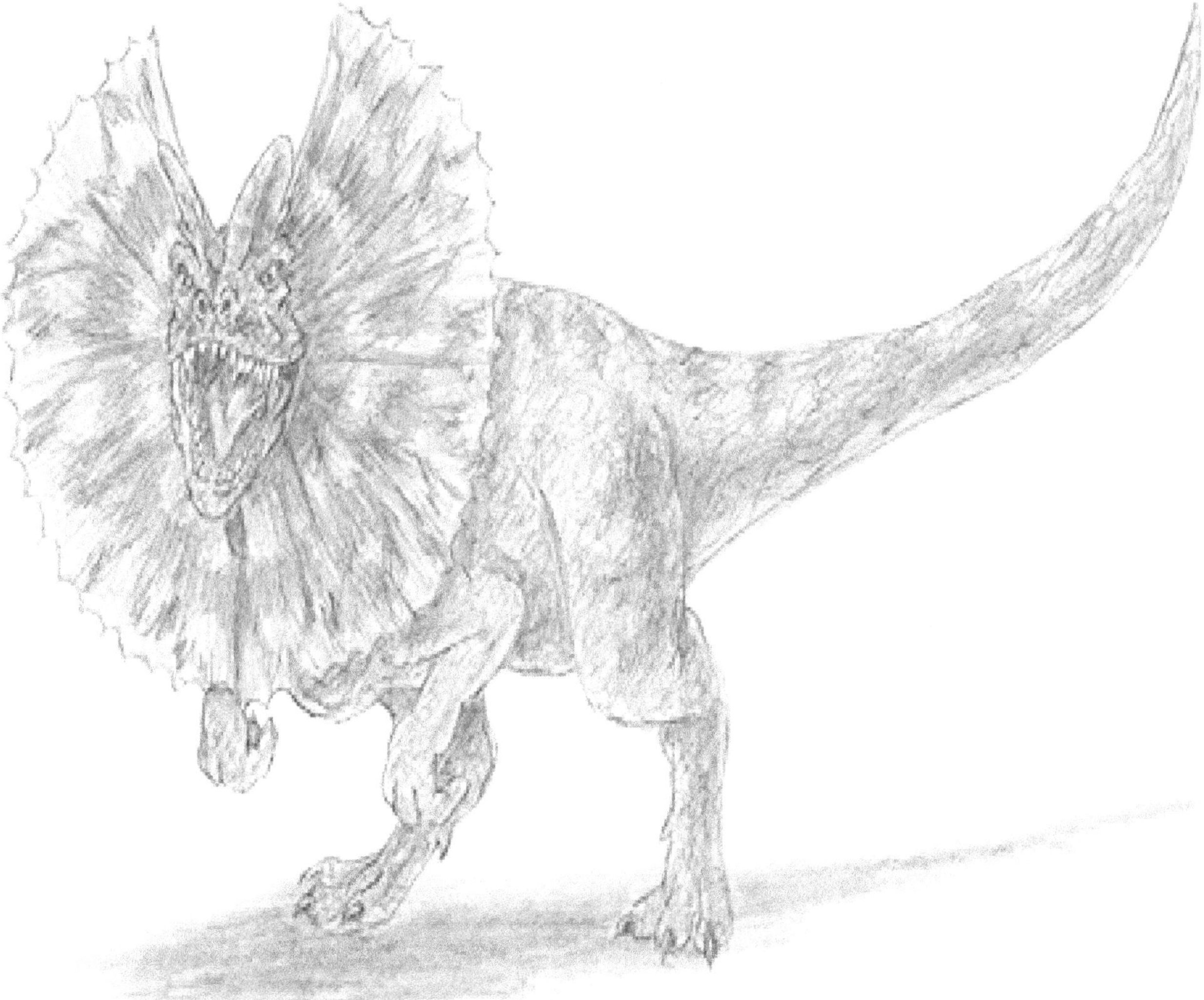

How to Draw an Allosaurus Dinosaur

Step 1:
Draw a circle near the middle of the page as a guide for the first part of the allosaurus' body. First draw four small marks to indicate the height and width of the circle, then connect the marks using curved lines. Sketch lightly at first so that it's easy to erase if you make a mistake. But the circle doesn't have to be perfect. It's just a guide. If you're struggling drawing the circle, trace the outer rim of a coin, a lid or any other object with a circular edge.

Step 2:

Draw another circle on the left the same way. Start by making four small marks. Then connect the marks using curved lines. This circle should be a bit bigger than the first one. Don't place the circles too far apart, otherwise your allosaurus will be too long.

Step 3:

Draw yet another circle on the right side as a guide for the first part of the dinosaur's head. This circle should be about half the size of the first one. Their edges should also touch.

Step 4:

Draw the guide for the top part of the allosaurus' mouth by first drawing a long sloping line to the right of the small circle. Now add a long line above it that curves downward where both lines meet.

Step 5:

Draw a similar shape at the bottom as the guide for the allosaurus' lower jaw. The basic shape consists of two sloping lines. This shape should also be thinner than the one above it.

Step 6:

Under the circle on the right, draw an angled line similar to the less -than sign (<) as a guide for the allosaurus' first arm. Add a short, diagonal line on the right as a guide for the other arm.

Step 7:

Under the circle on the left, draw an angled line similar to a warped letter Z as a guide for the dinosaur's first hind leg. To the left, draw another line for the other hind leg. This line should bend slightly a few times to indicate the joints.

Step 8:

Draw two short lines that connect the head to the body to create the neck. Draw two longer lines that connect the circles in the middle to finish the guide for the allosaurus' torso.

Step 9:

Draw the first part of the allosaurus' tail by attaching a long sloping line to the top, left side of the body. Now add a long line that slopes even more and attach it to the lower, left side of the body. Curve both lines so that they meet at the top and come to a point. You can also just draw the tip pointing straight back for an easier drawing. That's it for the initial sketch! From this point on, press harder with your pencil to get a more defined sketch.

Step 10:

Draw a small circle for the eye on the top, right side of the initial circle, on the outside. Sketch it lightly at first. When you get the placement and size right, darken the lines. Inside the allosaurus' eye, draw a tiny dot for the pupil. Add a few curved lines around the eye to emphasize the structure and the skin.

Step 11:

Draw the allosaurus' horn in front of the eye as an arc that's wavy and pointy. Sketch lightly at first to get the shape right, then darken the lines. This dinosaur's horns were small, so don't draw them to big. Add a similar shape to the left for the horn that's on the other side. Add a series of short lines within the shape to represent the bony texture.

Step 12:

Use the initial lines as guides to draw the top part of the open mouth. Follow the basic path of the guide, but make the lines wavier as you darken them for a more organic look. The line for the mouth at the bottom should be even wavier, and it should stretch to the left inside the circle. On the top, right side, add a few lines for extra detail on the dinosaur's skin and a small slit for the nostril.

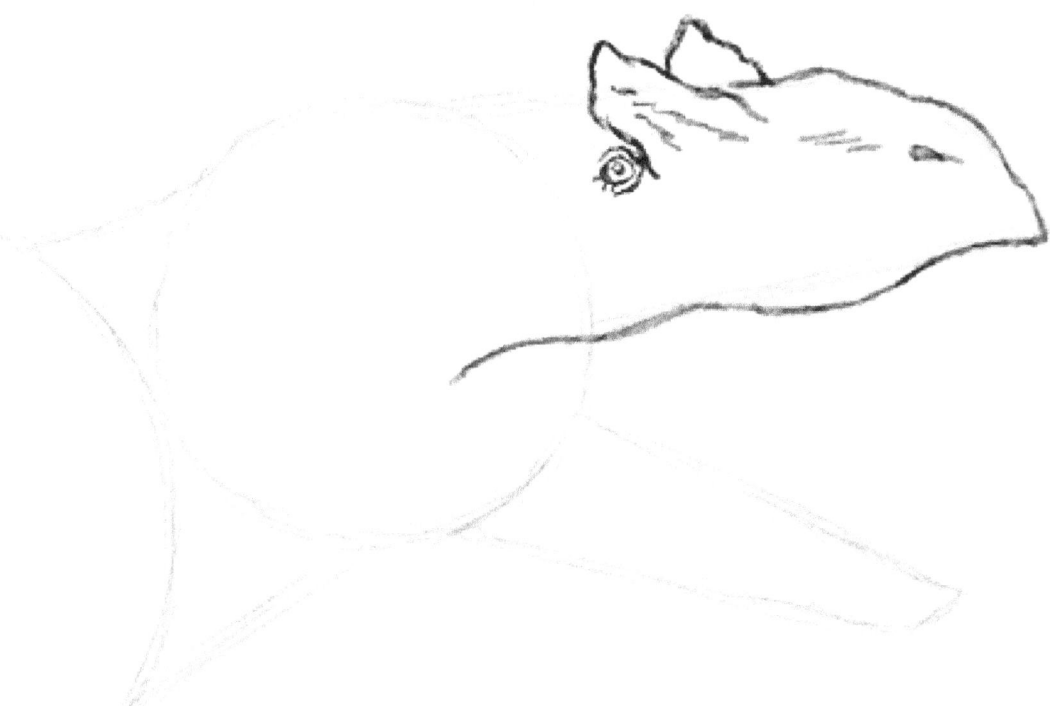

Step 13:

Now use the shape at the bottom as a guide to draw the allosaurus' lower jaw. Follow the path of the guide but make the line a lot wavier as you darken the line. Add a curved line on the left for the powerful jaw and a line in the corner of the mouth for the attaching skin.

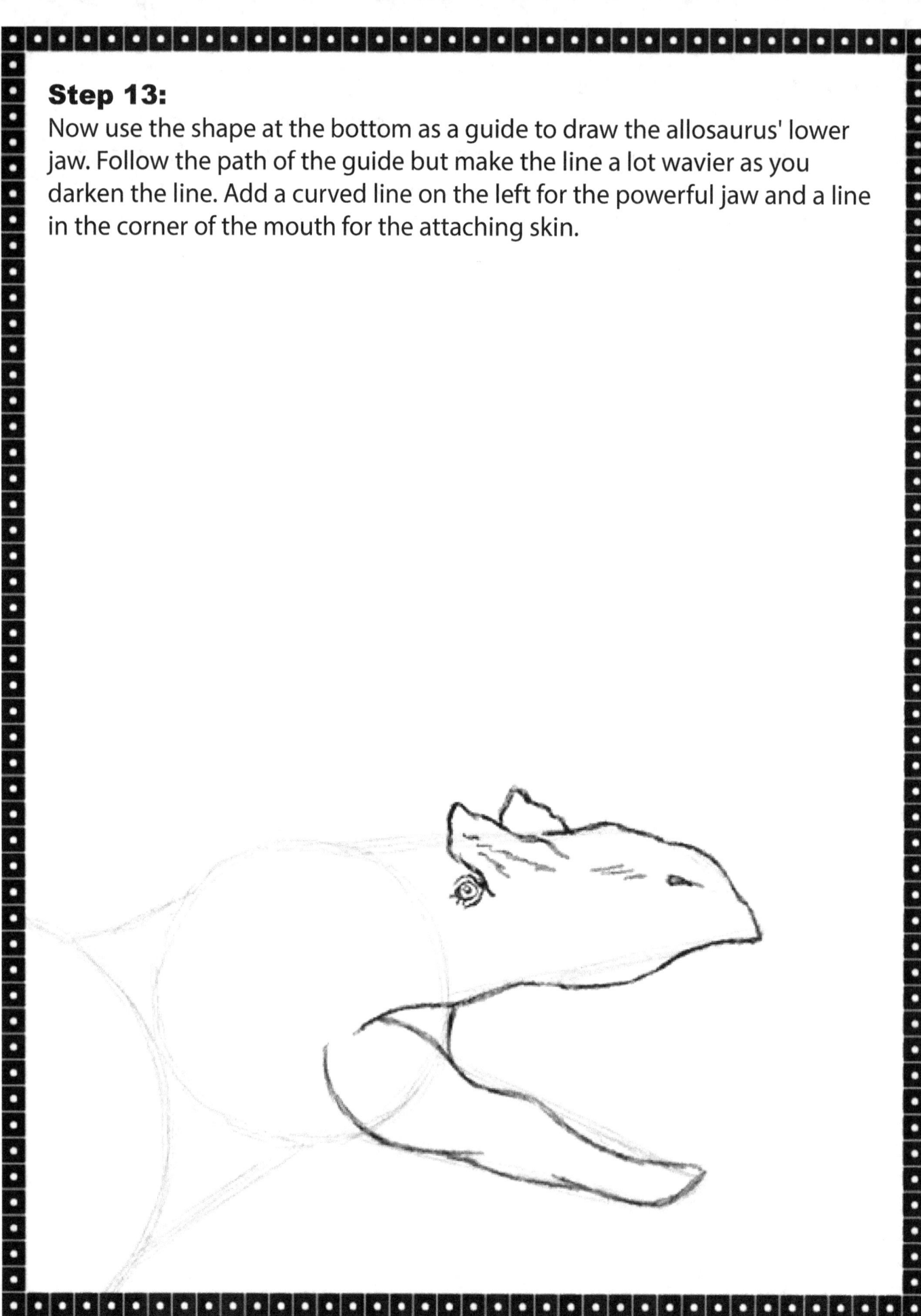

Step 14:

Draw a series of V-shaped lines along the top of the mouth for the dinosaur's teeth. Vary the size of the teeth a bit so that they don't all look exactly the same size. Now add the bottom row of teeth using more triangle-like, pointy shapes.

Step 15:

Draw the allosaurus' tongue in between the jaws, at the bottom, using a long wavy line. Add a couple of lines above and below the tongue for the other side of the jaw.

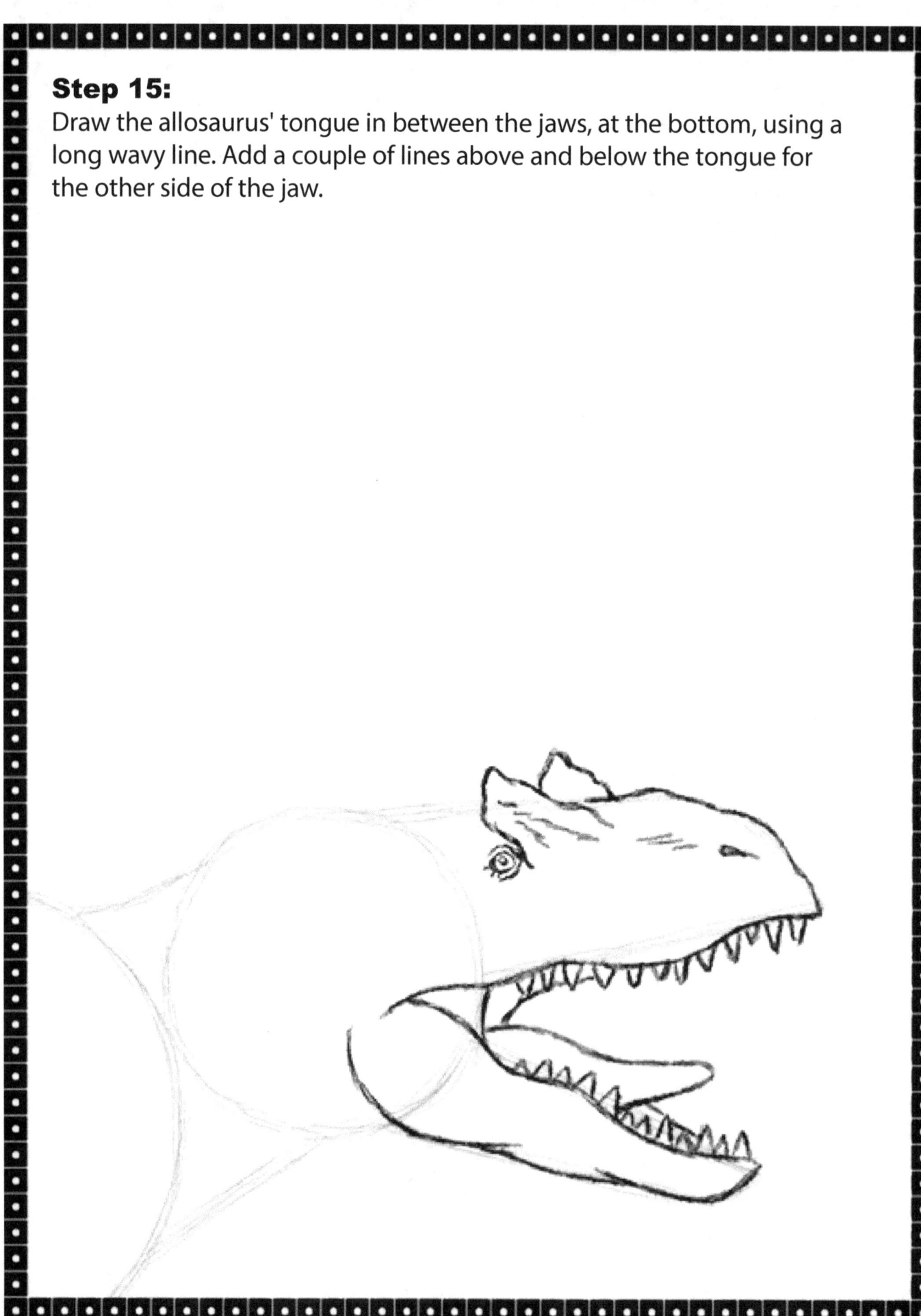

Step 16:

Use the remaining shapes and lines as guides to draw the rest of the head. Add a series of curved lines around the eye for the allosaurus' bony brow and darken the line on the left to create the back of the head. Darken the bottom edge of the guides to create the neck. Add a few triangle- like shapes along the head for spikes. Draw a few curved lines to the left of the eye to emphasize the cranial structure. Add a few more detail lines on the front part of the head. You can also omit these lines for a simpler drawing.

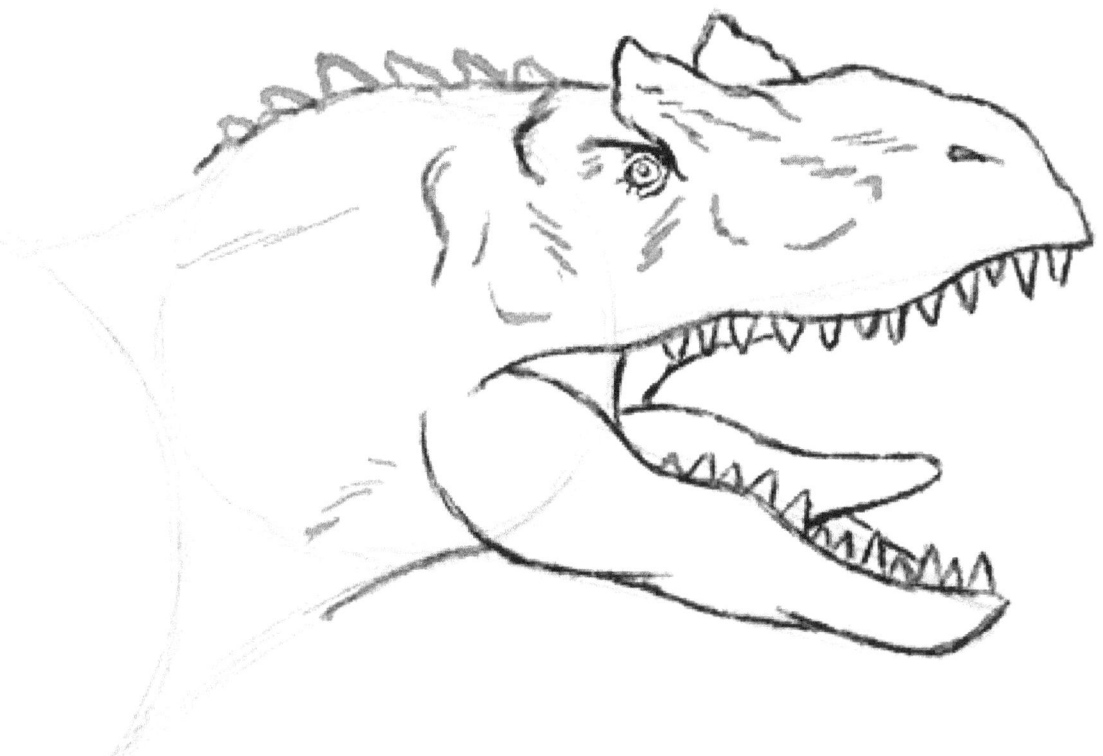

Step 17:

Use the second line from the right under the body as a guide to draw the first arm. Follow the path of the guide as you draw the shape of the arm around it. Use curved lines as you create the shape of the arm to give the muscles more definition. At the end of the arm, draw three short digits using thin, curved arcs. At the end of each digit, draw a short, curved, triangle-like shape for the dinosaur's claws.

Step 18:

Use the short line on the right as a guide to draw the other arm the same way. Draw the shape of the arm around the guide using curved lines.
The top part of the arm will be hidden behind the body. At the end of the arm, draw the three digits using curved arcs and the allosaurus' claws using triangle-like shapes.

Step 19:

Use the long, angled line in the middle as a guide to draw the allosaurus' first hind leg. Follow the basic path of the guide line as you draw the shape of the leg around it. Sketch the shape of the leg lightly at first. When you get all the curves and joints right, darken the lines. Add an extra curved line on the left of the leg near the middle for the pronounced muscle. The dinosaur's leg should be thick at the top. Draw the shape of the foot using the final segment of the angled line. Add the three long toes at the tip. The toes should overlap each other because of the perspective. Make the tips of the toes pointy for the claws.

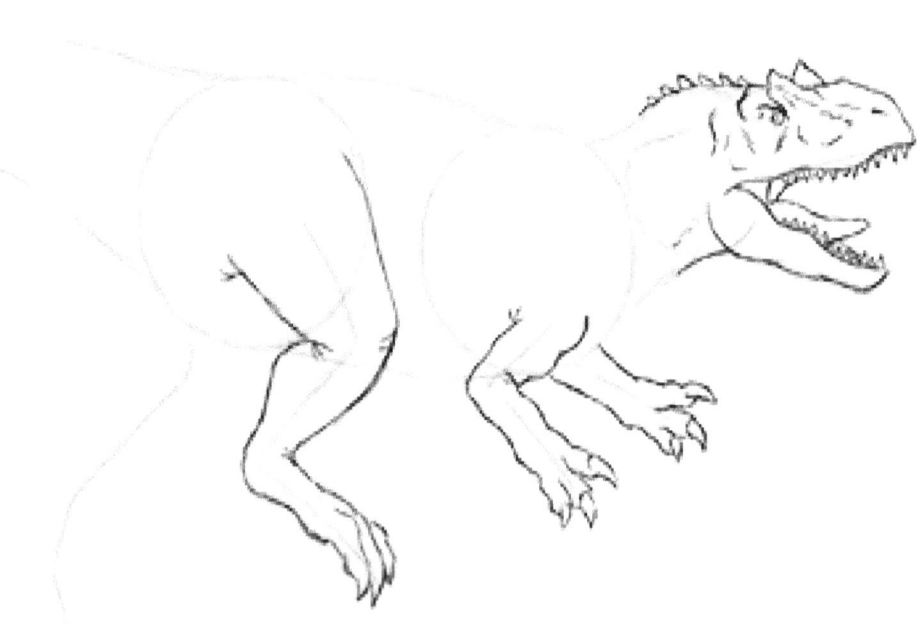

Step 20:

Use the leftmost line as a guide to draw the other hind leg. Follow the path of the guide and use a series of curved lines to represent the muscle structure along the leg. Add the pointy toes at the bottom. Notice that these toes look shorter than the ones on the other leg because they're bent. Follow the guide to draw the right edge of the leg. The shape of the allosaurus' leg should gradually get thicker near the top.

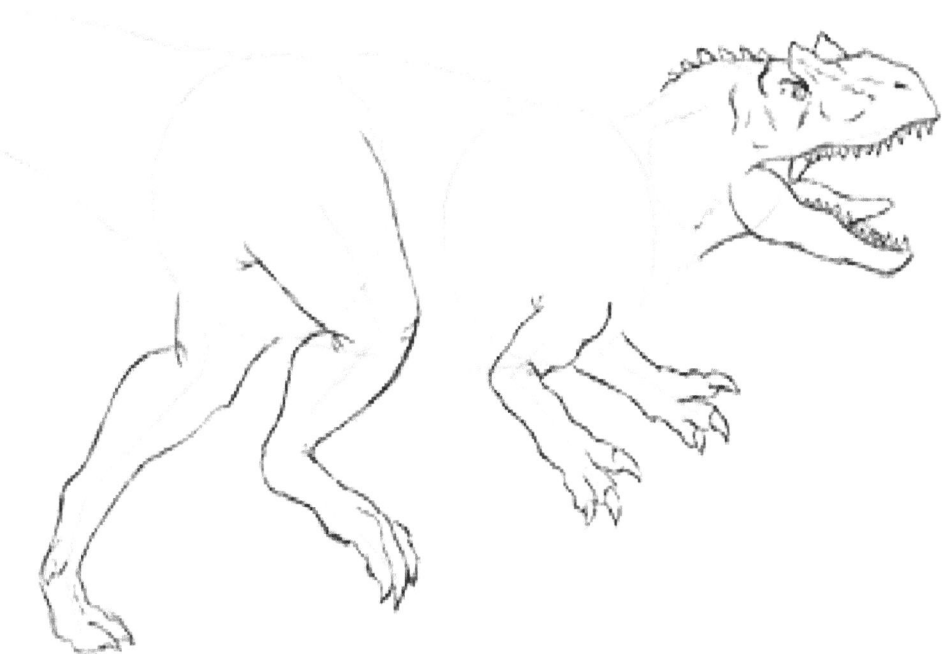

Step 21:

Use the initial lines and shapes as guides to draw the torso. Simply darken the outer edges of the initial guide line to create the shape of the body. Draw a series of small triangle-like shapes along the allosaurus' back for extra detail. Make the spikes different sizes for more variety. You can also omit them if you'd like.

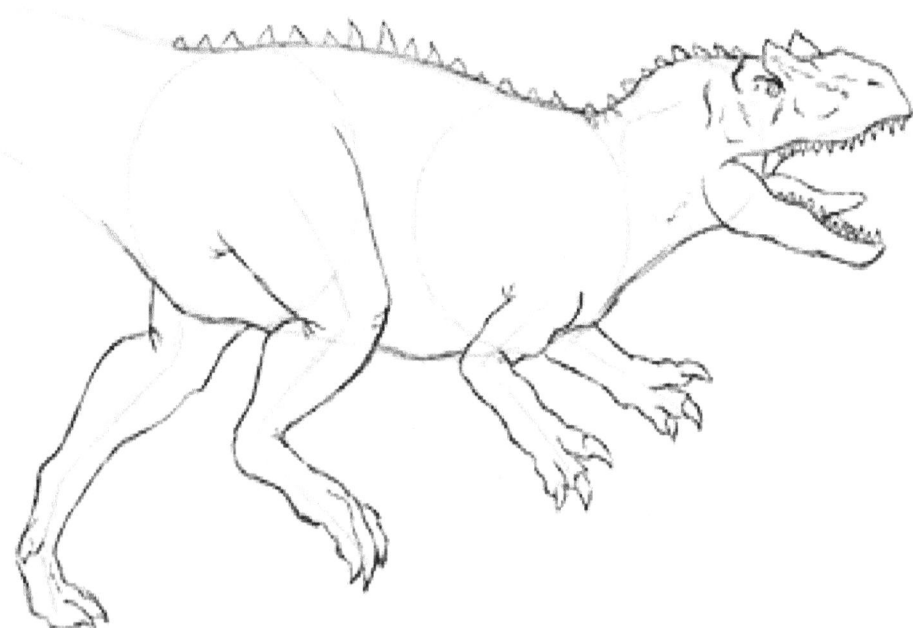

Step 22:

Darken the guides on the left for the allosaurus' tail. Add a few short spikes along the top edge of the tail too.

Step 23:

For a cleaner look, erase as much as you can of the initial guide lines. Don't worry about erasing all of the guides. It's okay to leave some behind. Re-draw any final sketch lines you may have accidentally erased.

Final Step:

Add some shading to your allosaurus drawing to give it more dimension and volume. Pick the direction of the light source when shading so that the shadows are consistent with it. Vary the pressure on your pencil to get different degrees of tonal value.Add a cast shadow underneath your allosaurus. This helps ground the dino so it doesn't appear to be floating.

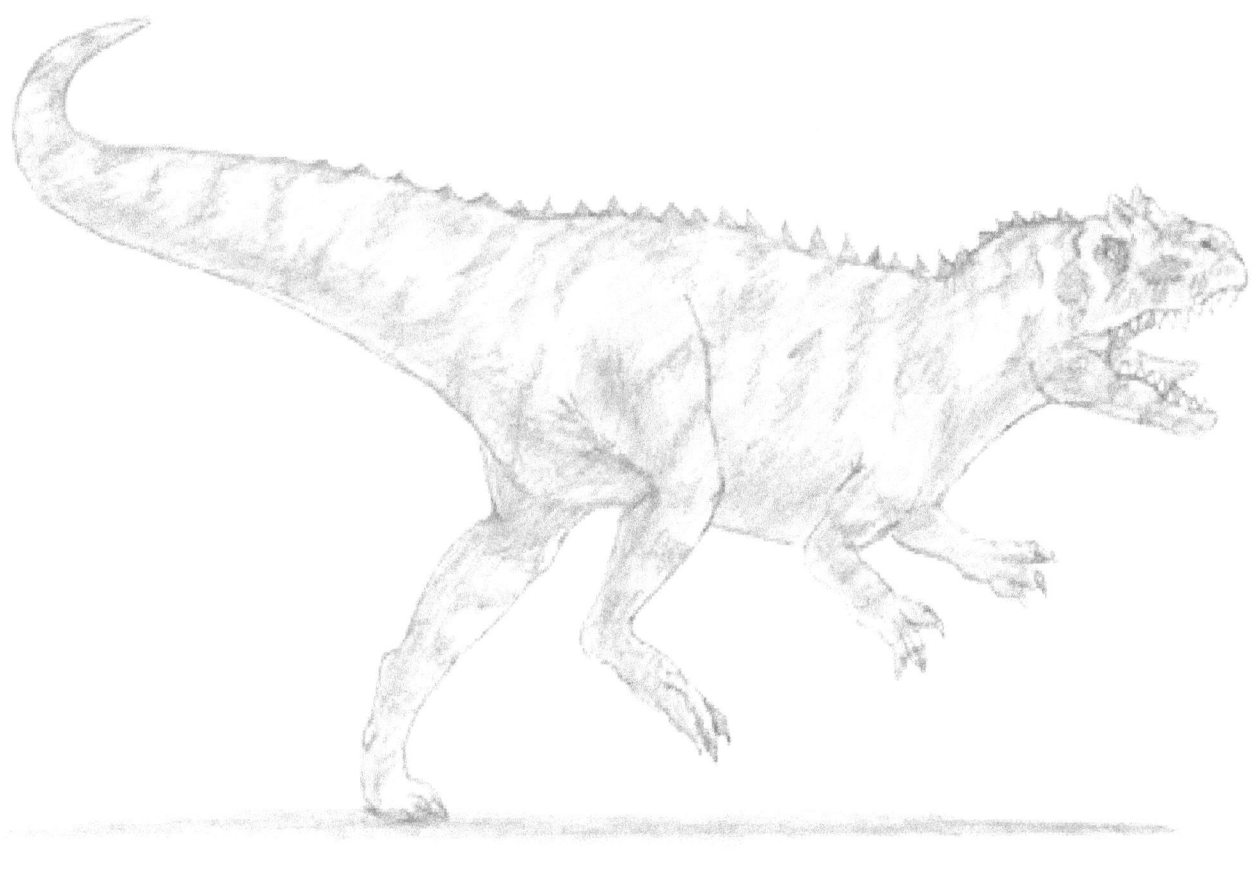

How to Draw an Indominus rex Dinosaur

Step 1:

Draw two circles as guides for the body of Indominus rex. The circles don't have to be perfect. They're just guides. The circle on the right should be bigger. The two circles should be close together. Leave enough room on the sides for the head and the tail.

Step 2:

Draw another circle on the upper left side as a guide for the Indominus rex's head. This circle should be a bit smaller than the first one, and their edges should touch.

Step 3:

Draw two arcs on the left side of the Indominus rex's head as guides for the open mouth. The top arc should be wider. The farther apart the arcs are from each other, the wider the open mouth will be.

Step 4:

Draw a series of curved lines that connect the major shapes to form the Indominus rex's body.

Step 5:

Draw two lines under the Indominus rex's body (below the circle on the right) as guides for the legs. Bend the lines to indicate where the joints will be. Space the lines apart to signify a step forward.

Step 6:

Draw another set of lines on the left side of the body as guides for the arms. Bend the lines to show where the joints will be and draw three smaller lines at the end to indicate the Indominus rex's digits.

Step 7:

Draw a couple of lines on the right side as a guide for the Indominus rex's tail. Curve the lines and have them come to a point on the right side. The longer they are, the longer the tail will be. That's it for the initial sketch! From this point on, press harder with your pencil to get a more defined sketch.

Step 8:

Draw the eye inside the Indominus rex's head, on the top left side, as a small football-like shape. Draw a thin slit inside the eye for the pupil. Shade the rest of the eye except for a tiny circle to represent glare. Add a few lines around the eye to indicate the bony structure. The eyes are set deep in the skull. The lines around the eyes create the indentation. Multiple curved lines create the wrinkly texture under the eye. Don't draw the lines too far down the head. They should basically form a circle around the eye. Add the bony brow ridge as a curved line over the eye.

Step 9:

Use the initial arcs as guides to draw the teeth lining the Indominus rex's mouth. Draw the teeth as small triangle-like shapes as you follow the path of the arcs. Randomly alternate between big teeth and little teeth. Indominus rex has teeth on the outside of the mouth similar to a crocodile.

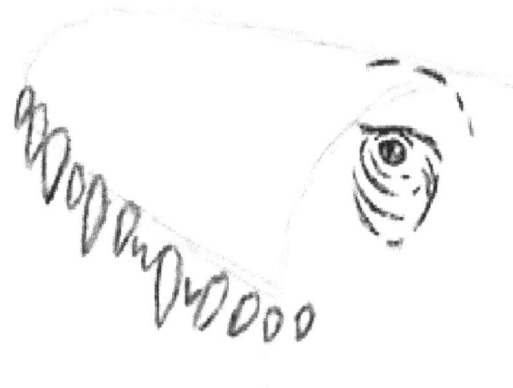

Step 10:

Use the top arc as a guide to draw the upper jaw. Follow the path of the arc and add a few bumps at the top and a slit at the front for the Indominus rex's nostril. Darken the line between the teeth. This line should stretch far to the right toward the back of the head.

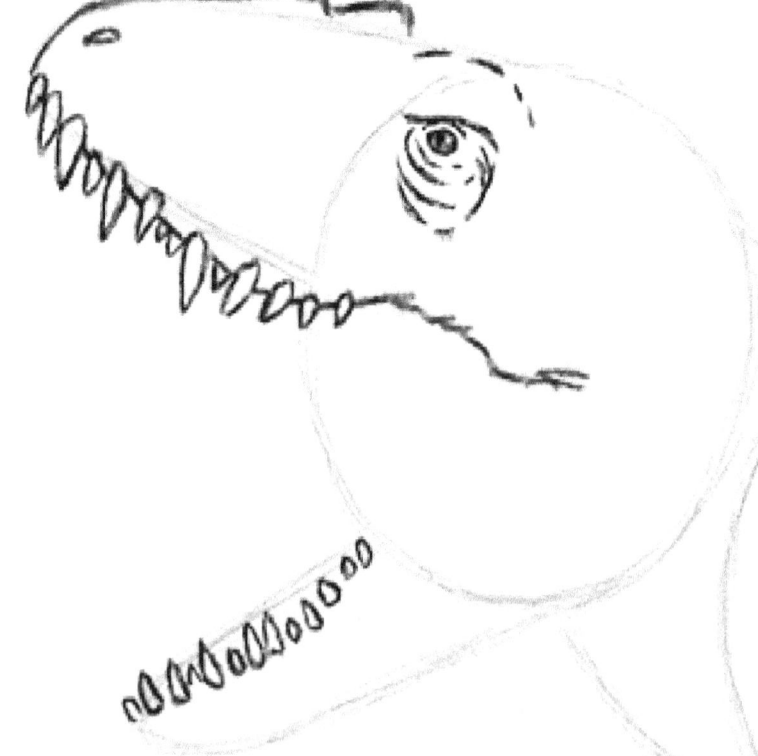

Step 11:

Draw the lower jaw by using the arc at the bottom as a guide. Follow the basic path of the arc as you darken the lines and add the lines between the teeth.

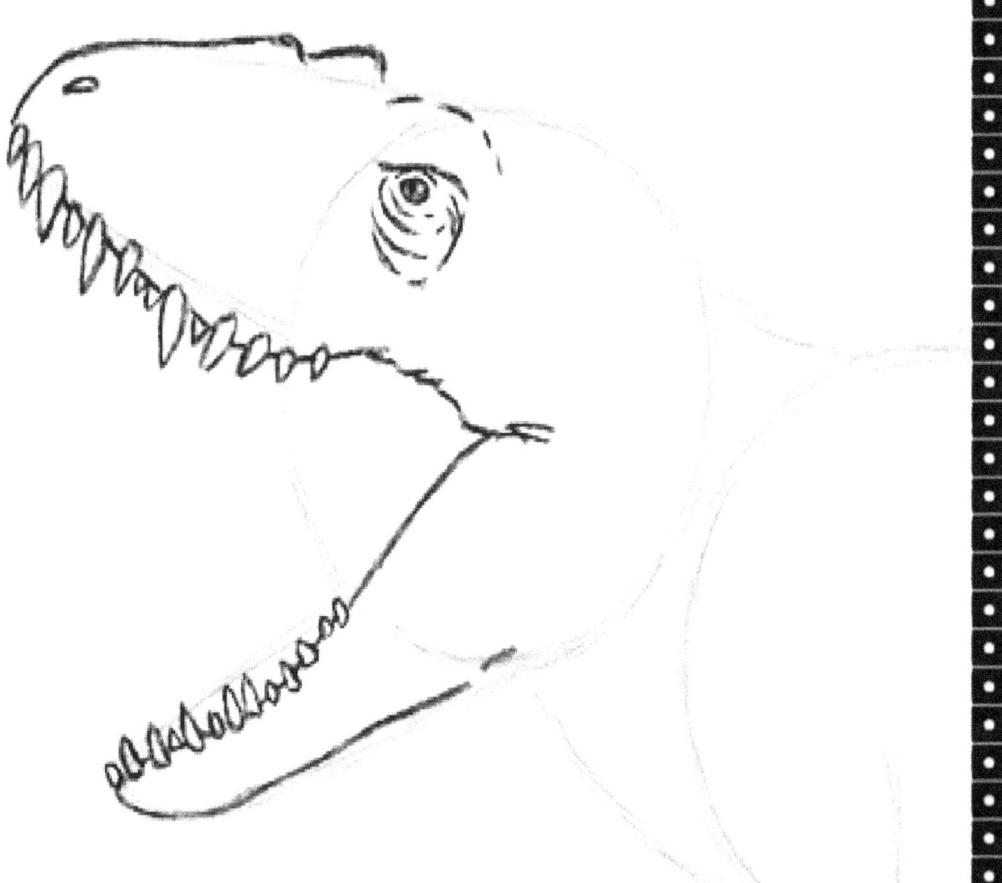

Step 12:

Draw the skin that attaches the top and bottom jaw as a series of lines. Draw the tongue as a curved line between the open mouth.

Step 13:

Draw the rest of the head using the initial shapes as guides. Follow the basic path of the guides as you draw the horn-like bumps on the Indominus rex's head. Add an oval-like shape in front and behind the eye for the indentations of the skull. Add a few small curved lines within the head for the bumpy skin texture. Add the spikes on the head as curved lines that come to a point.

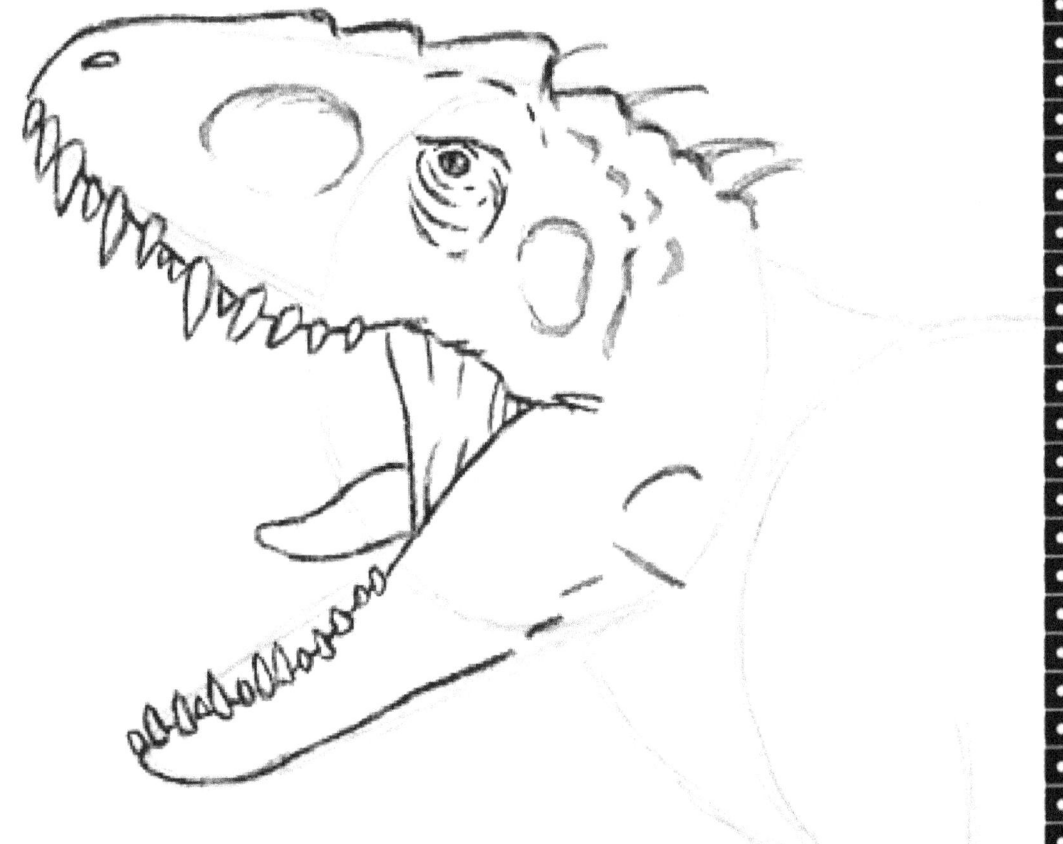

Step 14:
Use the line on the left side as a guide to draw the arm that's on this side of the body. Light sketch the shape of the arm as you follow the basic path of the guide line. Darken the lines when you get the structure of the Indominus rex's arm right. Use the small lines as guides to draw the digits and sharp claws. Add a few curved lines on the bottom edge of the arm for the spikes found there.

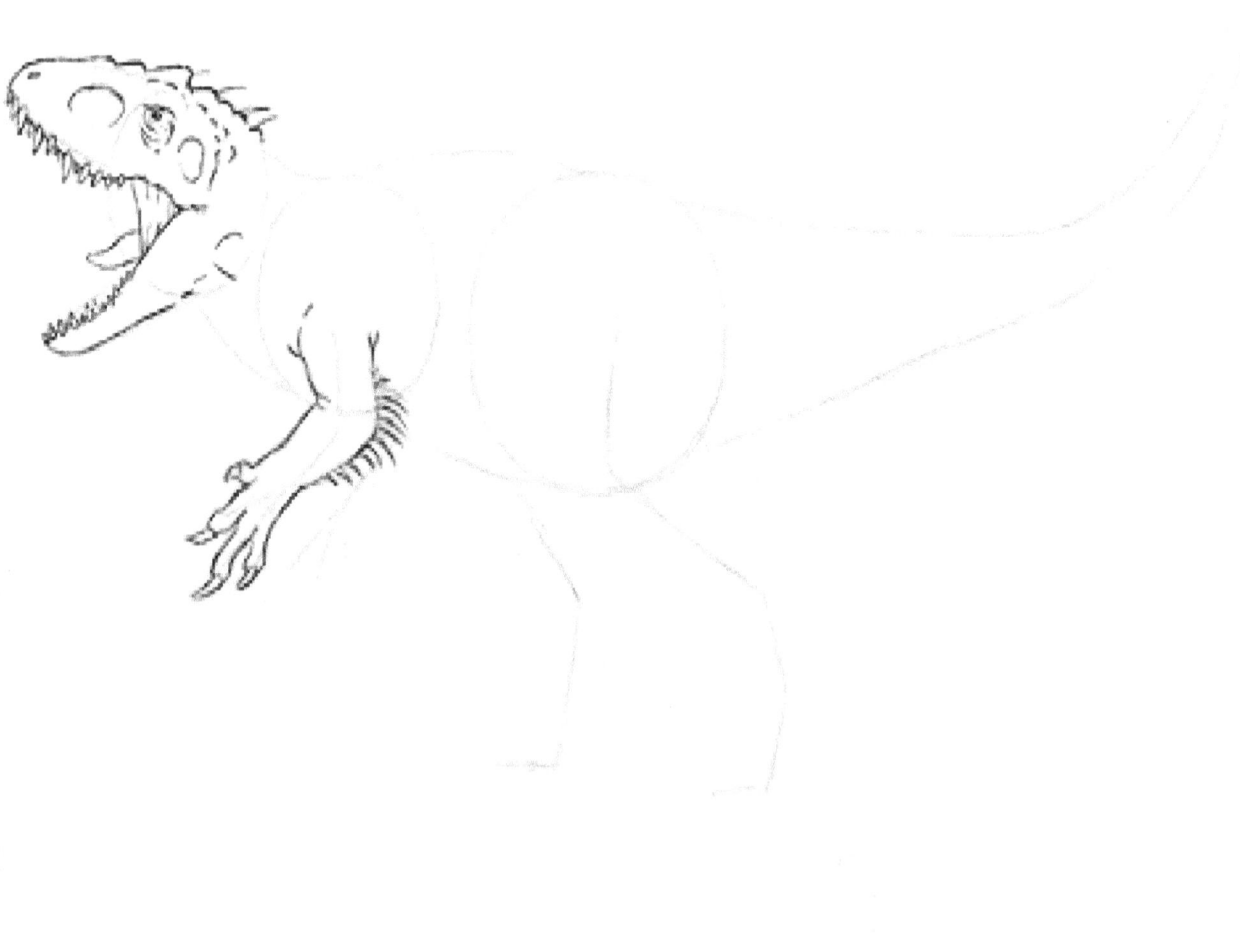

Step 15:

Use the other line on the left as a guide to draw the front arm on the other side of the Indominus rex's body. Part of the arm is blocked by the other arm and body, so don't draw the whole thing. Only the visible portion.

Step 16:

Use the line on the far right as a guide to draw the leg on this side of the Indominus rex's body. Sketch lightly as you follow the basic path of the guide. Use curved lines to indicate the leg muscles. Darken the lines only when you get the structure of the leg right. Draw the two toes and claws at the bottom that are visible from this angle. The leg should be thickest at the top and thinner at the bottom.

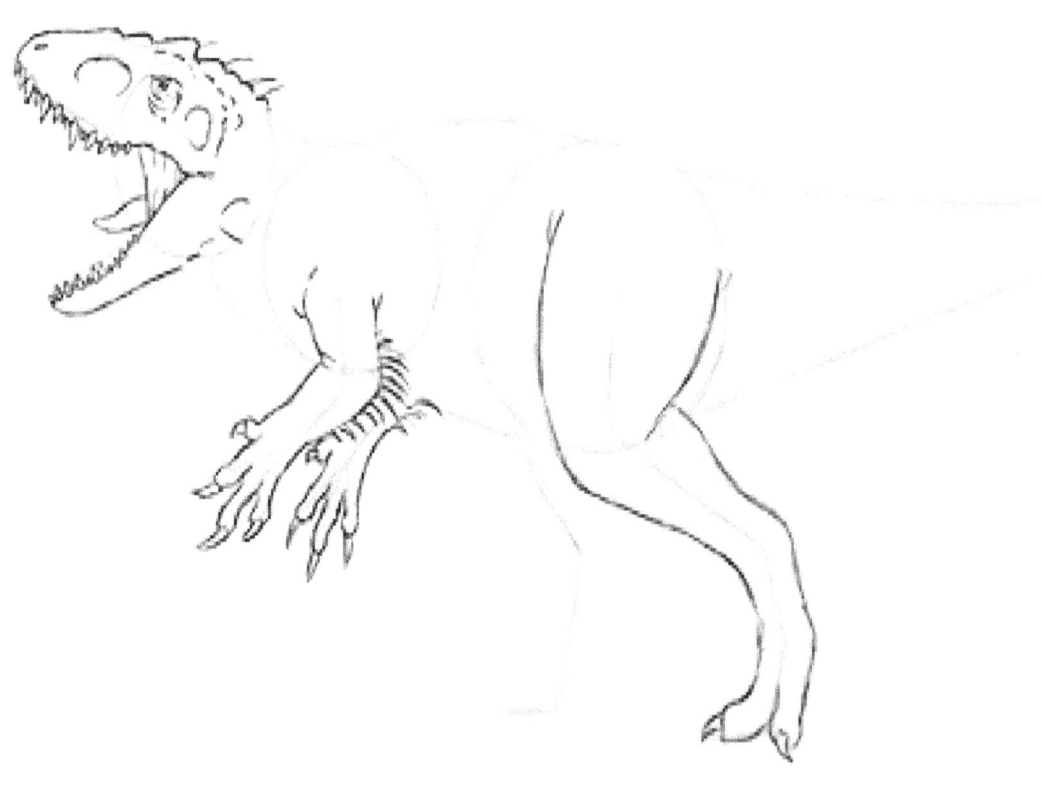

Step 17:

Use the last line at the bottom as a guide to draw the leg on the other side. Follow the path of the guide as you darken the lines and add the toes and claws at the bottom. Add the dew claw high on the side of the foot using a series of curved lines.

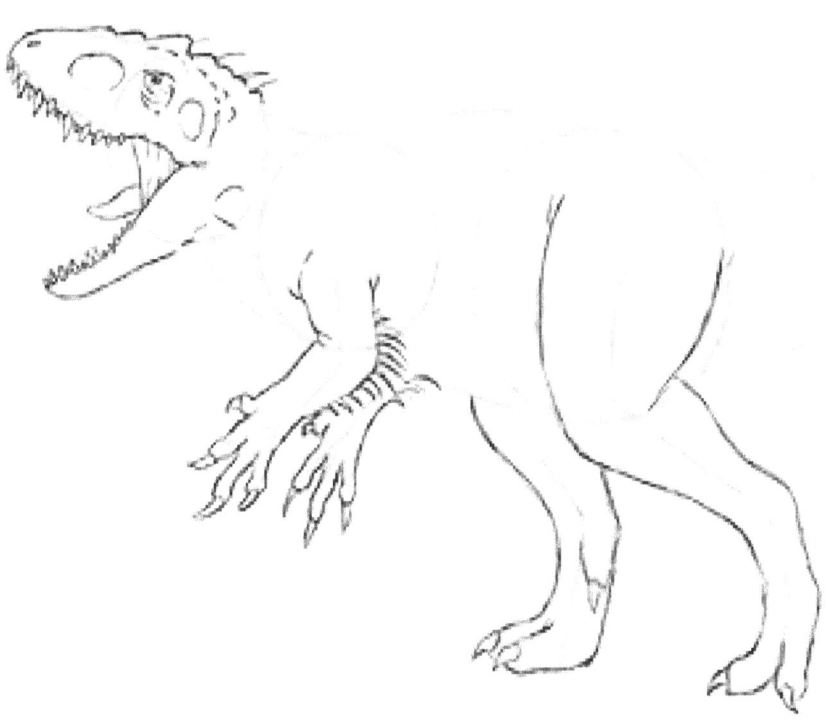

Step 18:

Use the initial lines and circles as guides to draw the Indominus rex's body. Use the small triangle-like shapes as you follow the path of the guides to create the bumps that line the back. Add some bumps within the shape of the body to create the crocodile-like texture on the back. Use the lines at the bottom as guides to draw the underside of the body.

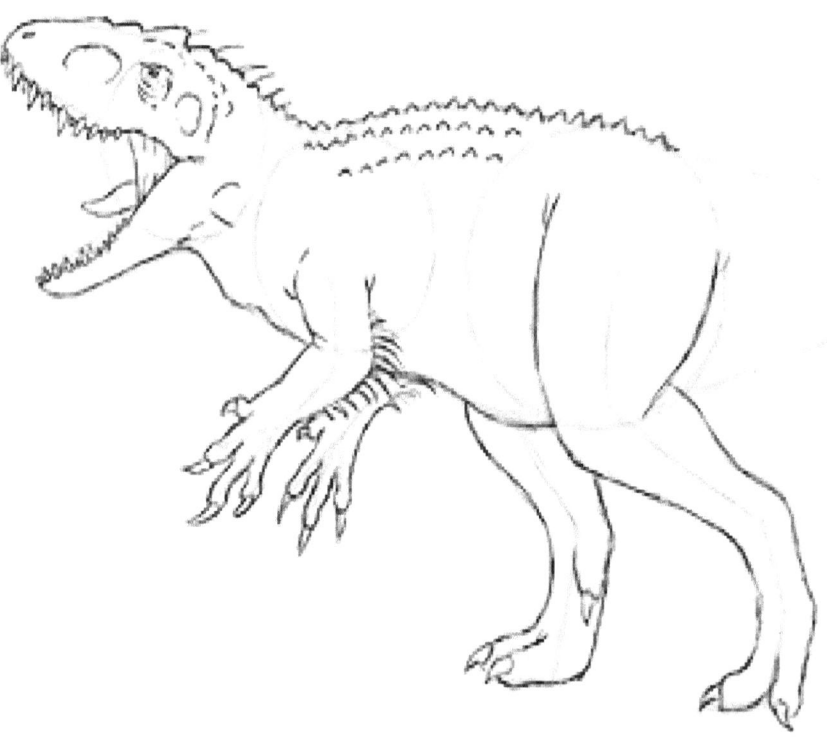

Step 19:
Use the lines on the right as guides to draw the Indominus rex's tail. Follow the path of the guides as you draw the small triangle-like spikes that line the top of the tail.

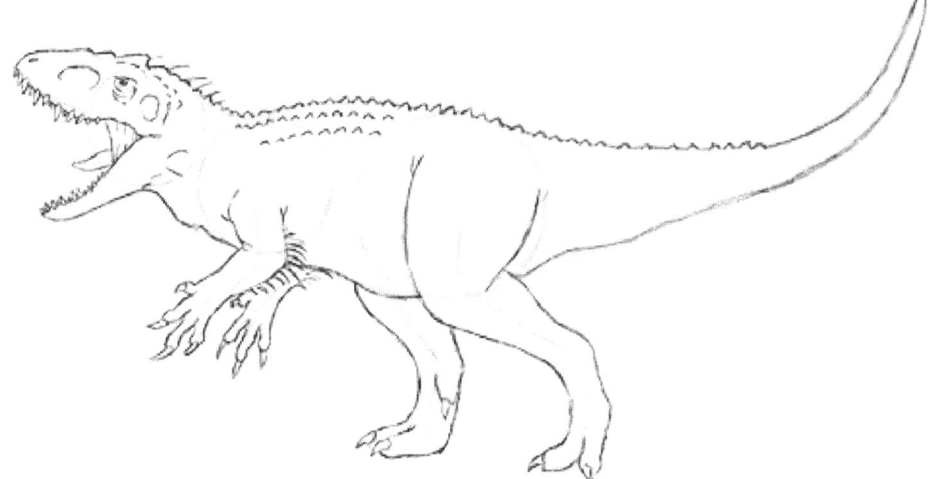

Step 20 (optional):

For a cleaner look, erase as much as you can of the initial guide lines. Don't worry about erasing all of the guides. It's okay to leave some behind. Re-draw any final sketch lines that you may have accidentally erased.

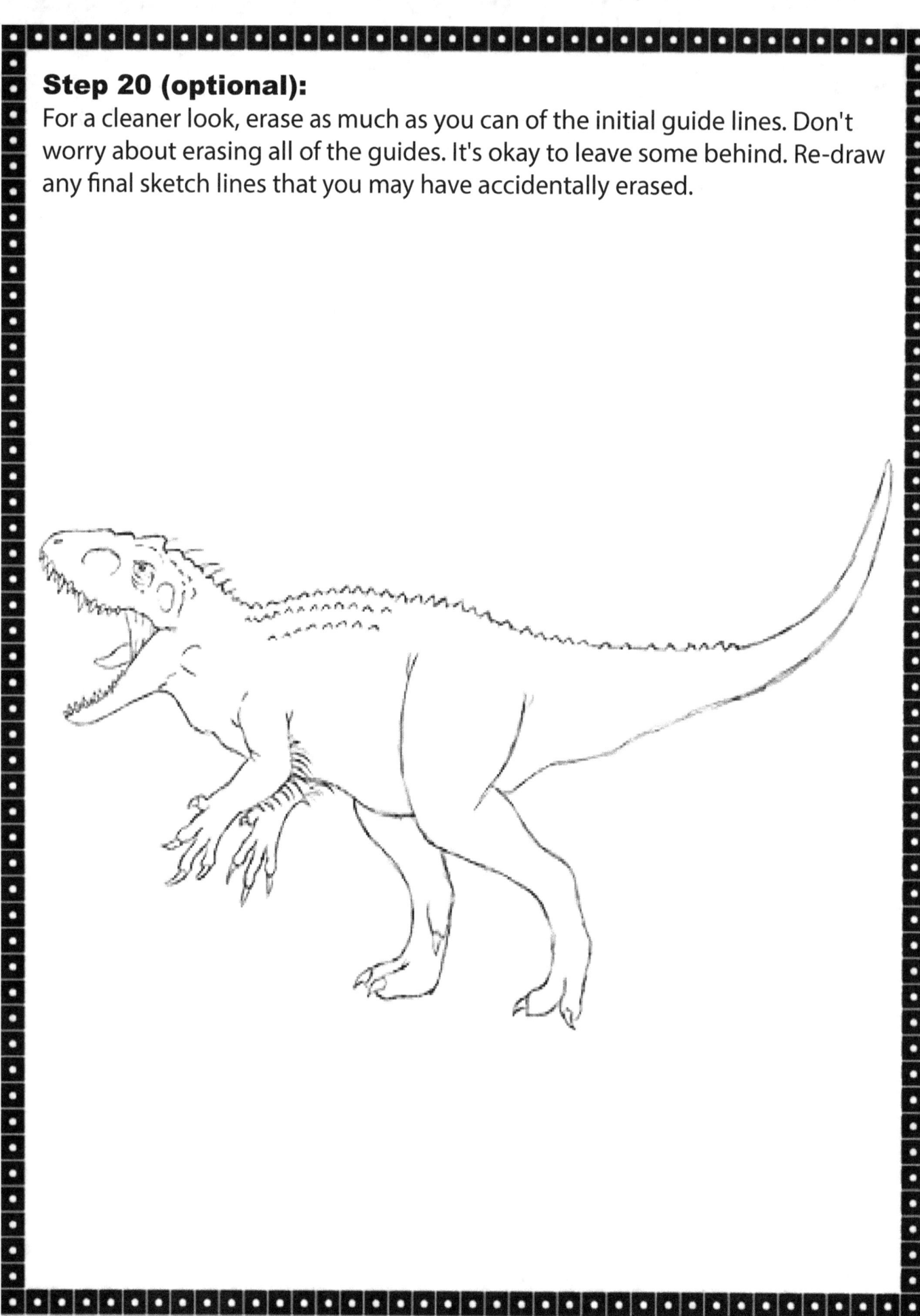

Final Step:

Add some shading to your drawing to give it more dimension and volume. The indentations created by the skull are deep, so add a dark value in the circles on the Indominus rex's head. Pick the direction of the light source when shading so that the shadows are consistent with it. Add the value lightly at first, then gradually build up to the level of darkness that you want. Vary the pressure on your pencil to get a different degrees of tonal value. Continue adding the value throughout the body to indicate the shadows. Draw a cast shadow underneath. This helps ground the dinosaur so it doesn't appear to be floating.

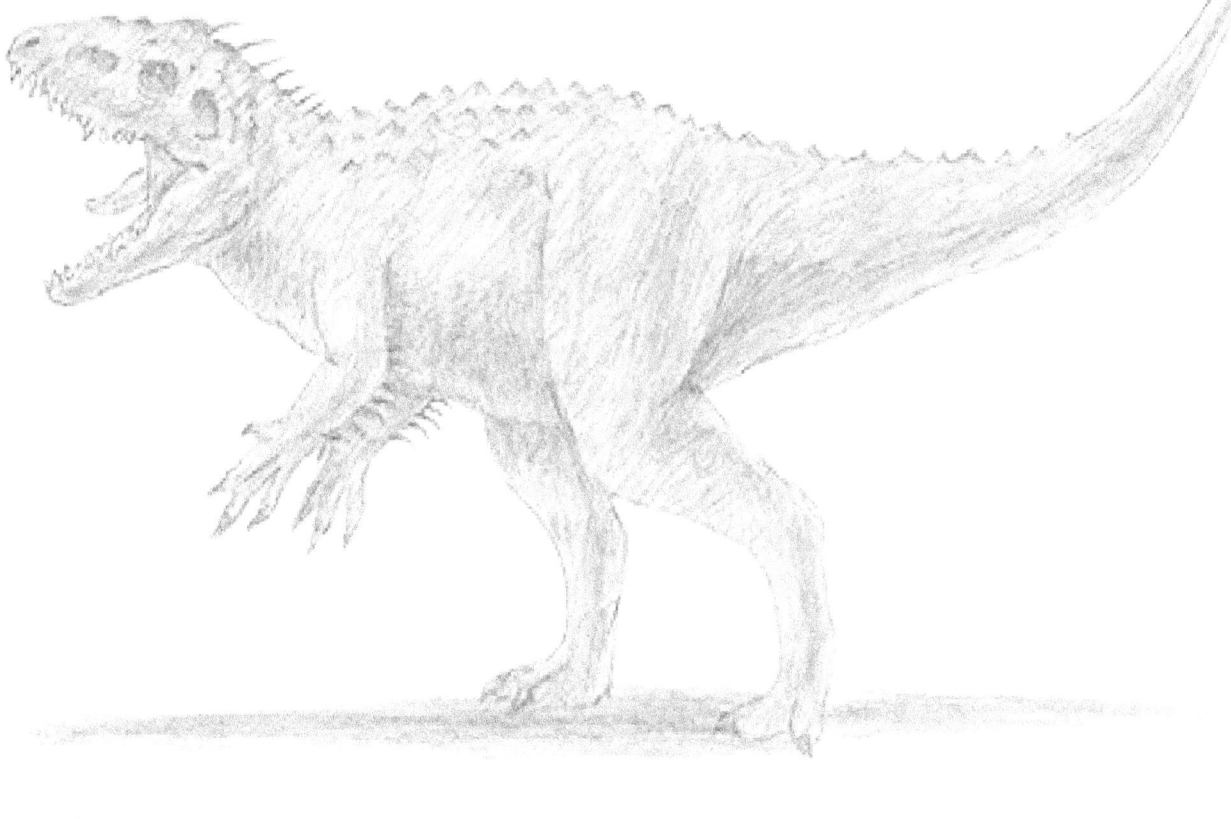

How to Draw a Dilophosaurus

Step 1:

Draw a half-circle on the left side as a guide for the top part of the Dilophosaurus' head. First draw a wide arc for the top part of the half-circle, then add a straight line under it for the bottom part. The half-circle doesn't have to be perfect. It's just a guide. Leave enough room on the sides for the rest of the dinosaur's body.

Step 2:

Draw two intersecting lines inside the Dilophosaurus' head to help you place the facial features later. Curve the lines a bit so that they contour to the shape of the half-circle.

Step 3:

Draw a long arc similar to the letter U under the head as a guide for the Dilophosaurus' lower jaw. The height of the jaw should be a bit longer than the height of the half-circle.

Step 4:

Draw a big circle around the head as a guide for the Dilophosaurus' open frill. First draw four marks around the head for the height and width of the circle. The marks should be about equal distance to the head. Now connect the mark using curved lines to complete the shape of the circle. Sketch the lines lightly at first so that they're easy to erase if you make a mistake. When you get the shape right, darken them. The bigger the circle is, the bigger the dinosaur's frill will be. It doesn't have to be perfect either. It's just a guide. If you do want a perfect circle, trace the outer rim of a glass, a lid or anything else that's circular.

Step 5:

Draw an angled line that looks similar to the number 7 on the lower right side of the big circle as a guide for the dinosaur's first arm. Pay attention to the size of this line in relation to the frill. Add an extra line at the bottom that makes it look like the letter Z. Draw a smaller angled line to the left as a guide for the Dilophosaurus' other front arm.

Step 6:

Draw a smaller circle to the right of the frill as a guide for the back portion of the body. The front part of the Dilophosaurus' body will be blocked by the frill, so don't worry about drawing a guide for it.

Step 7:

Draw another pair of angled lines under the circles as guides for the Dilophosaurus' legs. The first line shoud be basically vertical but should bend back near the middle for the joint before going down again. The other line should be similar to a greater-than sign (>). It's okay if the line overlaps with the line for the arm.

Step 8:

Draw a couple of long, curved lines to the right of the body as guides for the Dilophosaurus' tail. The first line should start on the top right side of the body and curve up until it's at the same height as the frill. The second line should start near the bottom of the body and meet the first line at the top to form a pointy tip. These lines should be about as long as the entire body. The longer you make them, the longer the dinosaur's tail will be.That's it for the initial sketch! From this point on, press harder with your pencil to get a more defined sketch.

Step 9:

Lightly sketch the Dilophosaurus' eyes inside the head, on the sides. Use the construction lines to help you with placement. The shapes of the eyes should be similar to half-circles that are slightly tilted. When you get the position and shape of the dinosaur's eyes right, darken the lines.Draw a short, diagonal line over each eye for the Dilophosaurus' heavy brow. Inside each eye, draw a small dot for the pupils. Add a tiny circle off to the side to represent glare. Add a small curved line under each eye for the lower eyelid. Draw a wavy line high above each eye for the bony outer structure. Add a line below each eye too so that the bony structure envelopes the eyes.

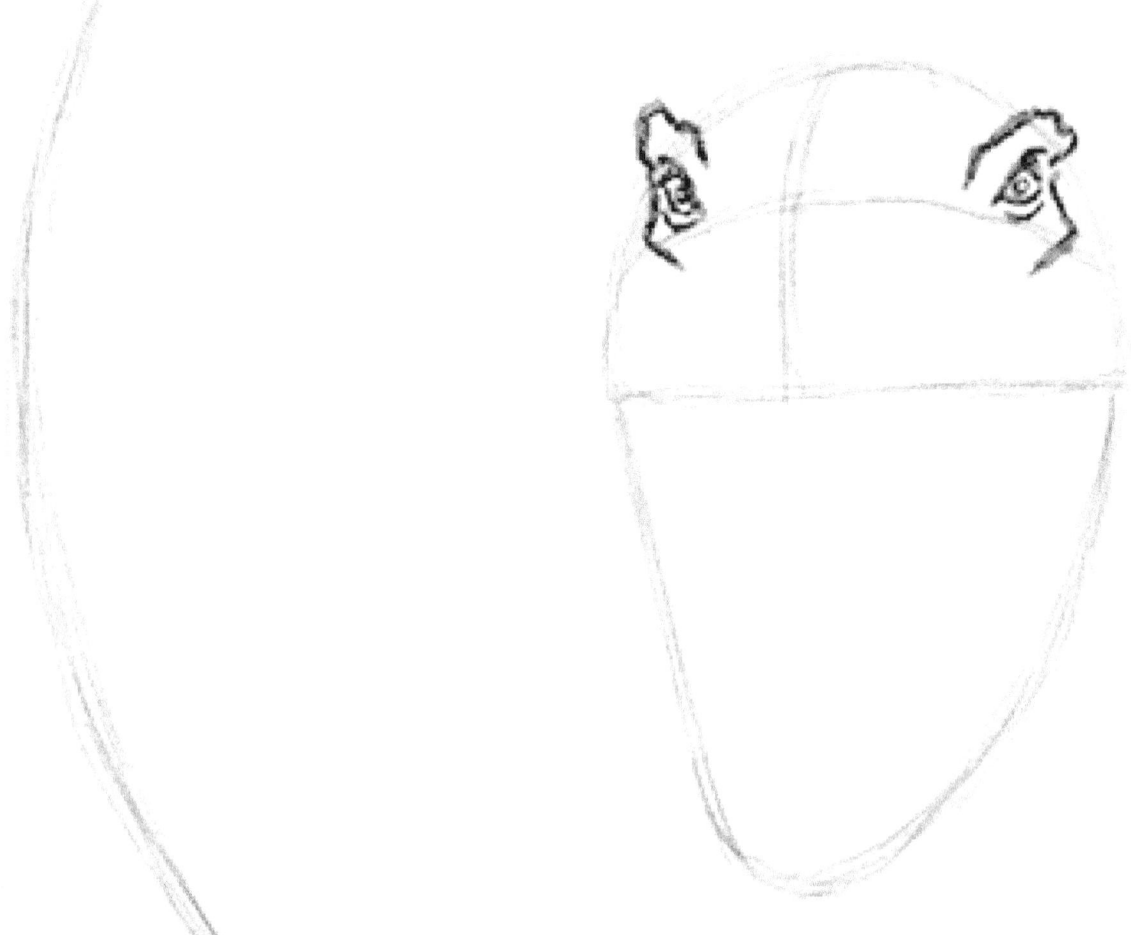

Step 10:

Draw the crest on the right by first lightly sketching an arc that's slightly tilted. Pay attention to the angle and the height and width of the arc. When you get it right, darken the lines. Make the outline of the Dilophosaurus' crest a bit jagged and add an extra line within it to indicate the curvature of the shape.

Step 11:

Lightly sketch another arc on the left side of the head that's tilting the opposite way for the Dilophosaurus' other crest. Draw a line in the middle of the arc, then darken the outline of the crest using a jagged line. Draw a few more lines near the bottom of the arc to indicate the shape turning away from the first arc.

Step 12:

Draw two small curved lines under the horizontal construction line for the top ridge of the Dilophosaurus' nose. Draw two small triangle- like shapes under the small, curved lines and shade them in for the actual nostrils. Add a few more lines around the dinosaur's nostrils to emphasize the structure.

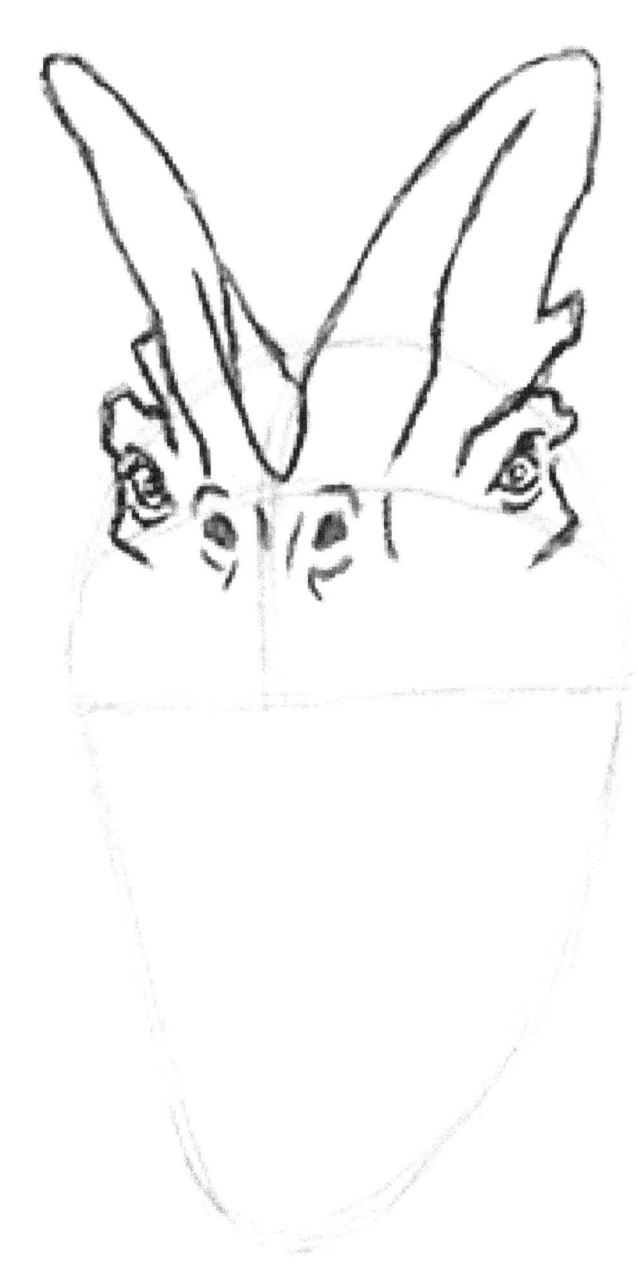

Step 13:

Use the bottom part of the initial half-circle shape as a guide to draw the Dilophosaurus' top jaw. Follow the basic path of the guide but curve the section in the middle more and place it a bit higher than the guide. The sides of the top jaw should curve down below the guide. Add a few more lines within the shape of the top jaw to give it more structure.

Step 14:

Draw a series of long triangle-like shapes directly under the top jaw for the Dilophosaurus' top row of teeth. Follow the path of the jaw as you draw the teeth. Make them different sizes to add variety. The row of teeth shouldn't stretch all the way to the sides of the top jaw.

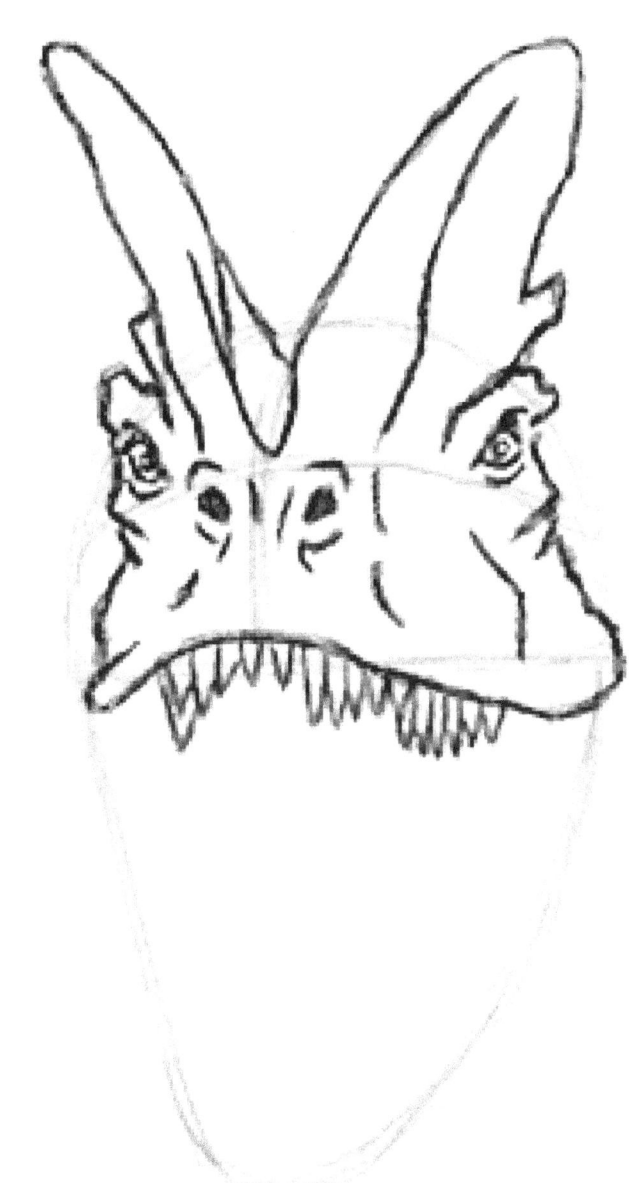

Step 15:

Use the curved line under the head as a guide to draw the Dilophosaurus' lower jaw. Follow the basic path of the guide but make the shape of the jaw a bit more jagged as you darken the lines. Inside, draw another line that has a similar shape but smaller for the open mouth. Use the lower jaw as a guide to draw the shape of the dinosaur's open mouth. Leave a big enough space to draw the inside detail.

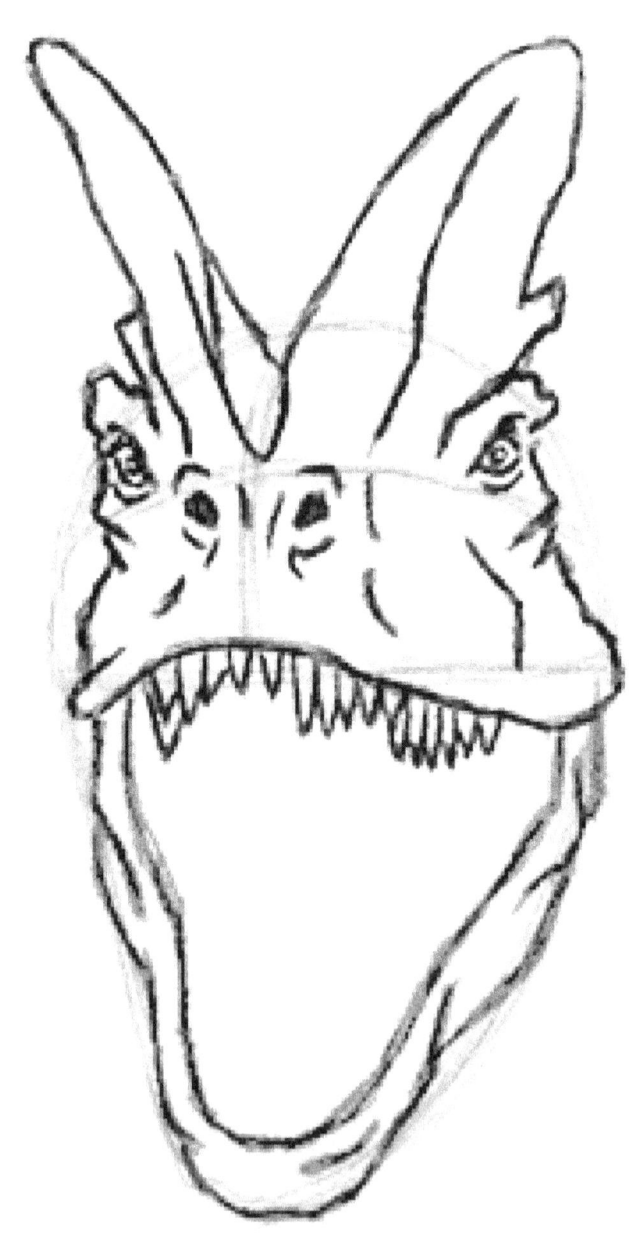

Step 16:
Draw a few short lines on the sides of the mouth for the skin in between the jaws. Draw a series of small triangle-like shapes that line the bottom of the Dilophosaurus' mouth for the teeth.

Step 17:

Draw a series of curved lines inside the Dilophosaurus' mouth for the tongue. The tongue should come to a rounded point at the bottom. Add some lines on the sides for the dinosaur's throat.

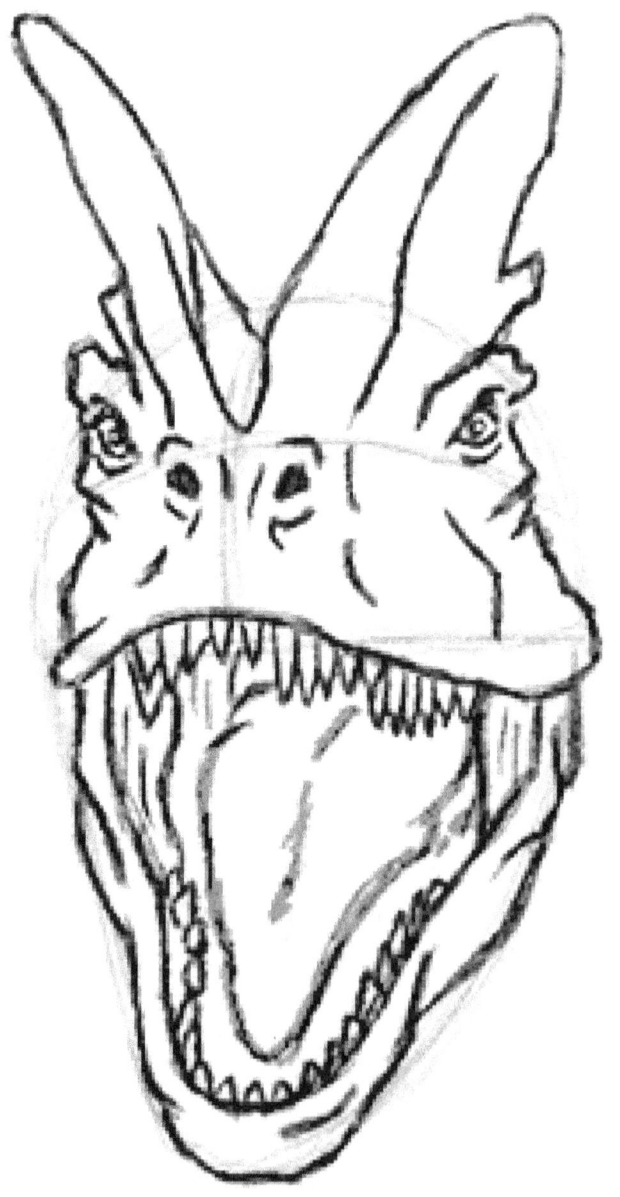

Step 18:

Use the big circle around the head as a guide to draw the right part of the Dilophosaurus' open frill. First draw a diagonal line at the top of the head and a vertical line at the bottom to separate the two sides of the frill. Now follow the path of the circle as you draw a series of small curved lines to give the frill a spiky appearance. You can make the shape of the frill come out of the circle a bit so as to not make the shape too perfect. Vary the size of the small curved lines to make the spikes different sizes for a more organic feel.

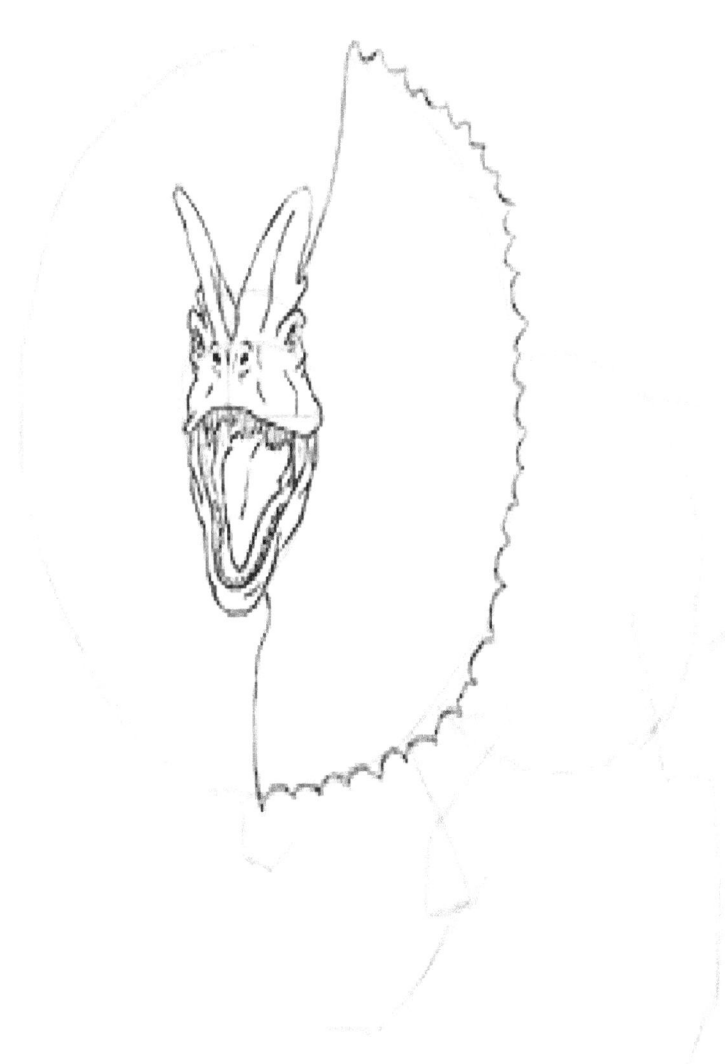

Step 19:

Draw another diagonal line above the head for the top part of the frill on the left side. Then add the series of small curved lines as you follow the path of the circle to make the Dilophosaurus' frill spiky. Make the curved lines different sizes to vary the sizes of the spikes.

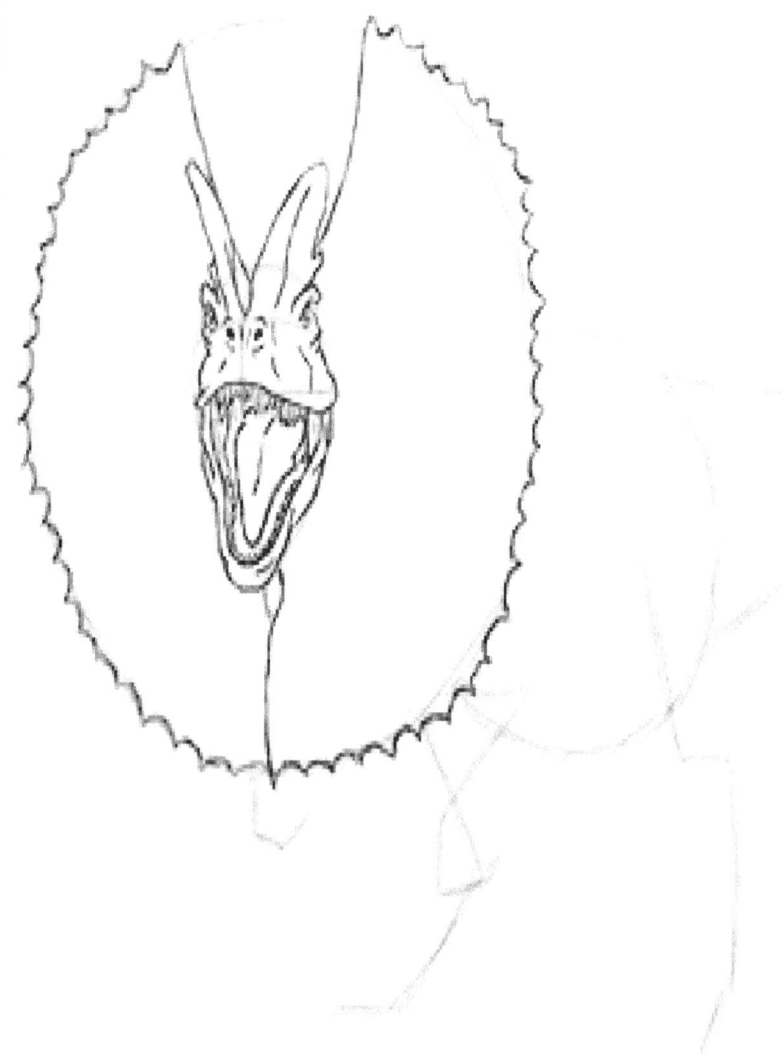

Step 20:

Add a few lines within the shape of the frill for the folds of the skin. As you draw these, lines make sure to angle them correctly so that they radiate from the middle of the Dilophosaurus' head. The lines in the middle should be horizontal then become more diagonal as they move up and down on the frill until they're almost vertical.

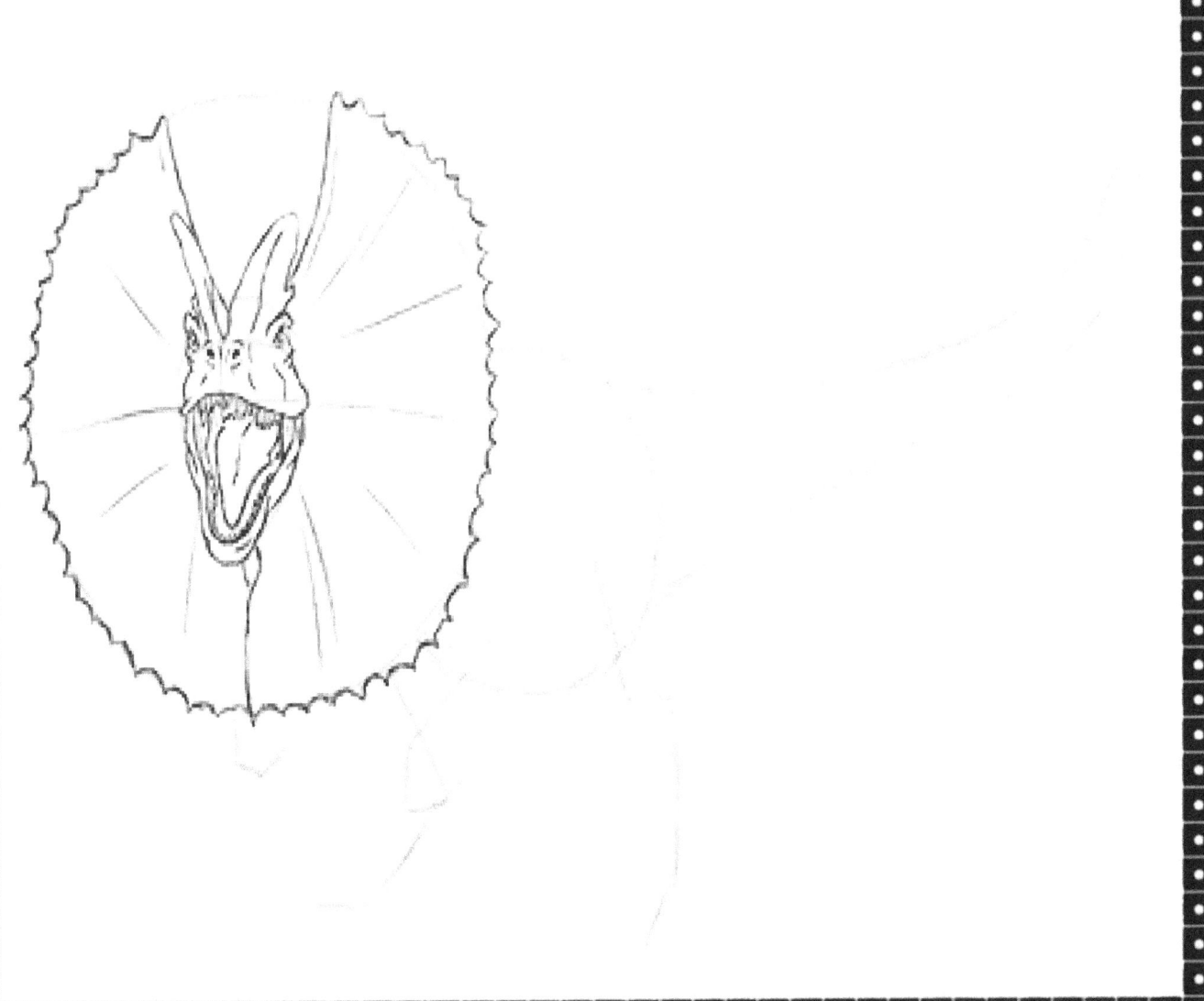

Step 21:

Use the angled lines under the frill as guides to draw the Dilophosaurus' arms. Follow the path of the guide shaped like a Z as you make the top part of the arm thicker. The arm is folded back toward the body. The top of the arm will overlap the bottom as it bends at the joint. The three digits also curve backward, so add three short curved lines at the bottom for the dinosaur's knuckles. Most of the digits are hidden behind the hand, but add the small visible one on the right side as a curved line. Draw the Dilophosaurus' hand on the other side using the other anged line as a guide. The digits should point backward, so add a few curved lines on the right side of the hand for the visible digits.

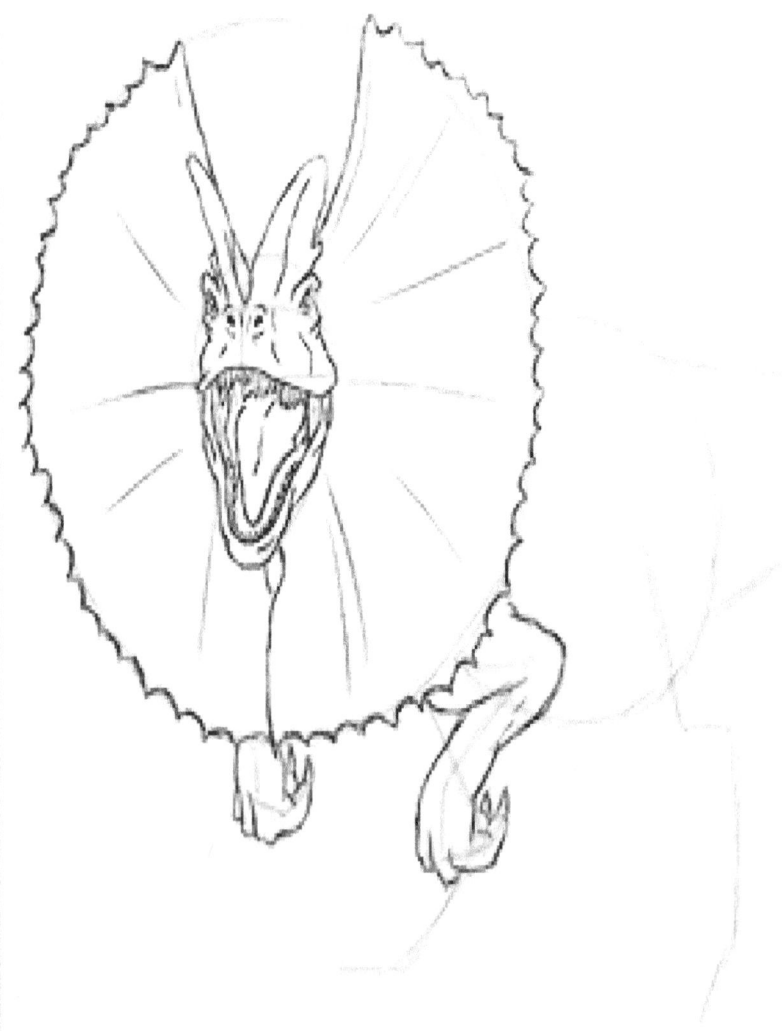

Step 22:

Use the angled line on the right as a guide to draw the Dilophosaurus' hind leg that's on this side of the body. Use long curved lines to make the top part of the leg thick. It should take up a big portion of the body. The bottom part of the dinosaur's leg should be thinner and placed off to the right so that the thicker top part appears to be in front of it. Add a small dewclaw near the middle of the bottom part of the leg and start adding the toes at the bottom. Draw three curved lines at the bottom for the Dilophosaurus' toes. The toe on the right should point to the right while the other two should point down. On the tip of each toe, draw a short, curved spike for the sharp claw. Draw the visible part of the other hind leg using the initial line as a guide. Draw the long middle toe and claw first. This foot is facing sideways, so not all three toes are visible. Just draw two and the small dewclaw. Don't overlap the lines for the dinosaur's hand and arm. The hind leg should be behind them.

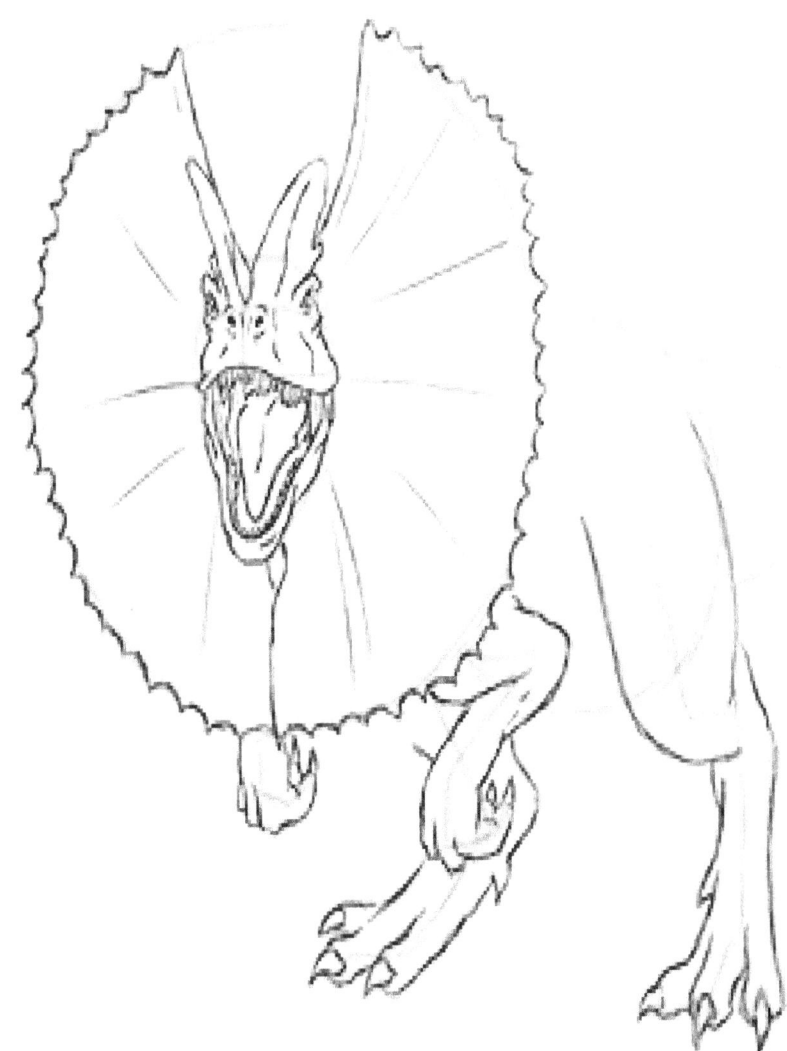

Step 23:

Use the remaining guides to draw the rest of the Dilophosaurus' body. Start by adding a curved line under the frill for the loose skin or dewlap. Then darken the outer path of the initial guides to create the shape of the body. Darken the lines for the dinosaur's tail too. The tail should point up to counter balance the front part of the body and the head.

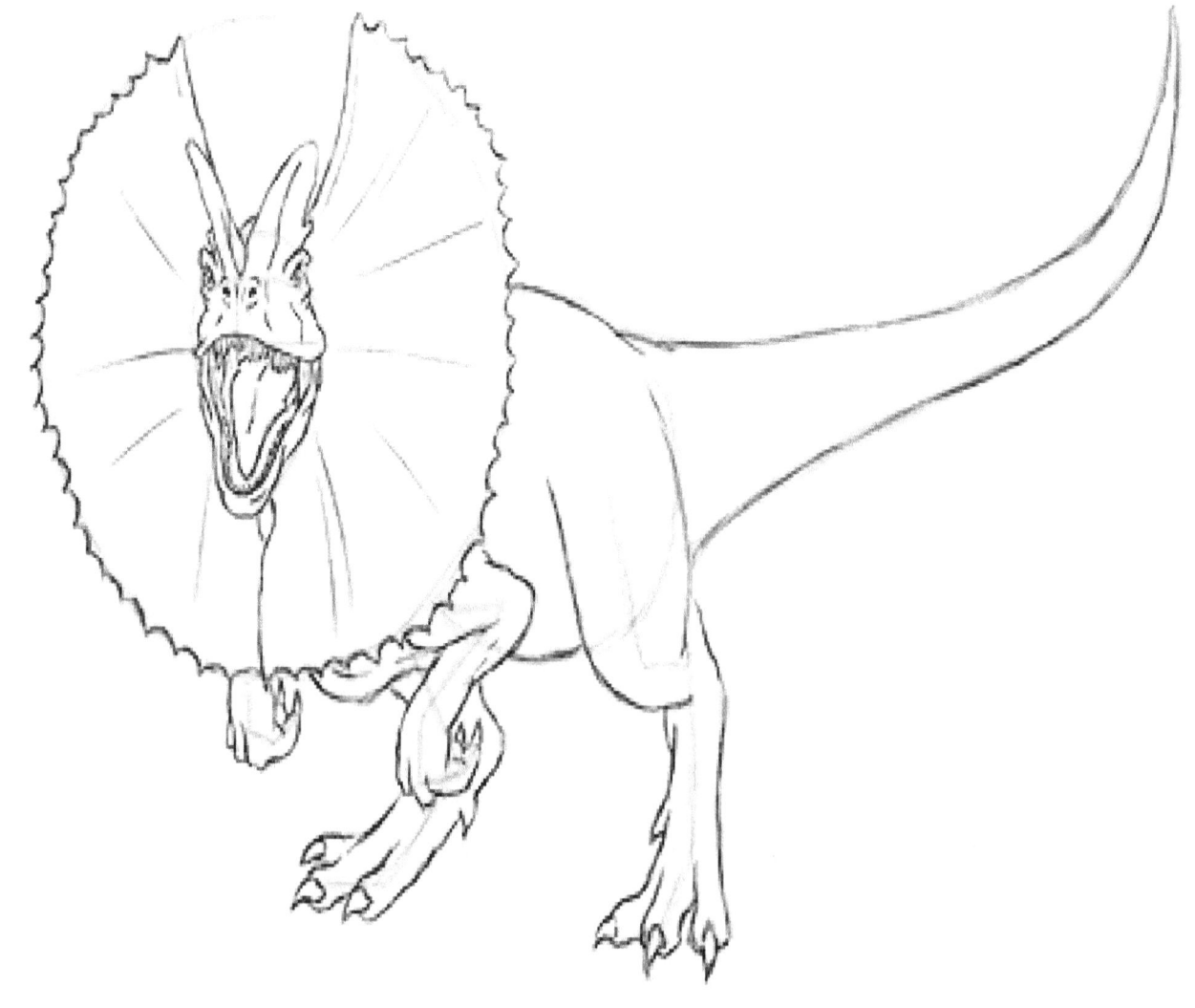

Step 24 (optional):

For a cleaner look, erase as much as you can of the initial guide lines. Don't worry about erasing all of the guides. It's okay to leave some behind. Re-draw any final sketch lines that you may have accidentally erased.

Final Step (optional):

Add some shading to your Dilophosaurus drawing to give it more dimension and volume. The inside of the mouth should be especially dark. As you shade the frill, use strokes that radiate from the center of the head toward the outer edge of the frill. Follow the path of the lines inside the frill as you shade. You can turn the paper around to make it easier. Pick the direction of the light source when shading so that the shadows are consistent with it. Vary the pressure on your pencil to get different degrees of tonal value. Add a cast shadow underneath your Dilophosaurus dinosaur. This helps ground the dino so it doesn't appear to be floating. Use a darker value near the middle of the shadow and a lighter value along the edge for the shadow's diffusion.

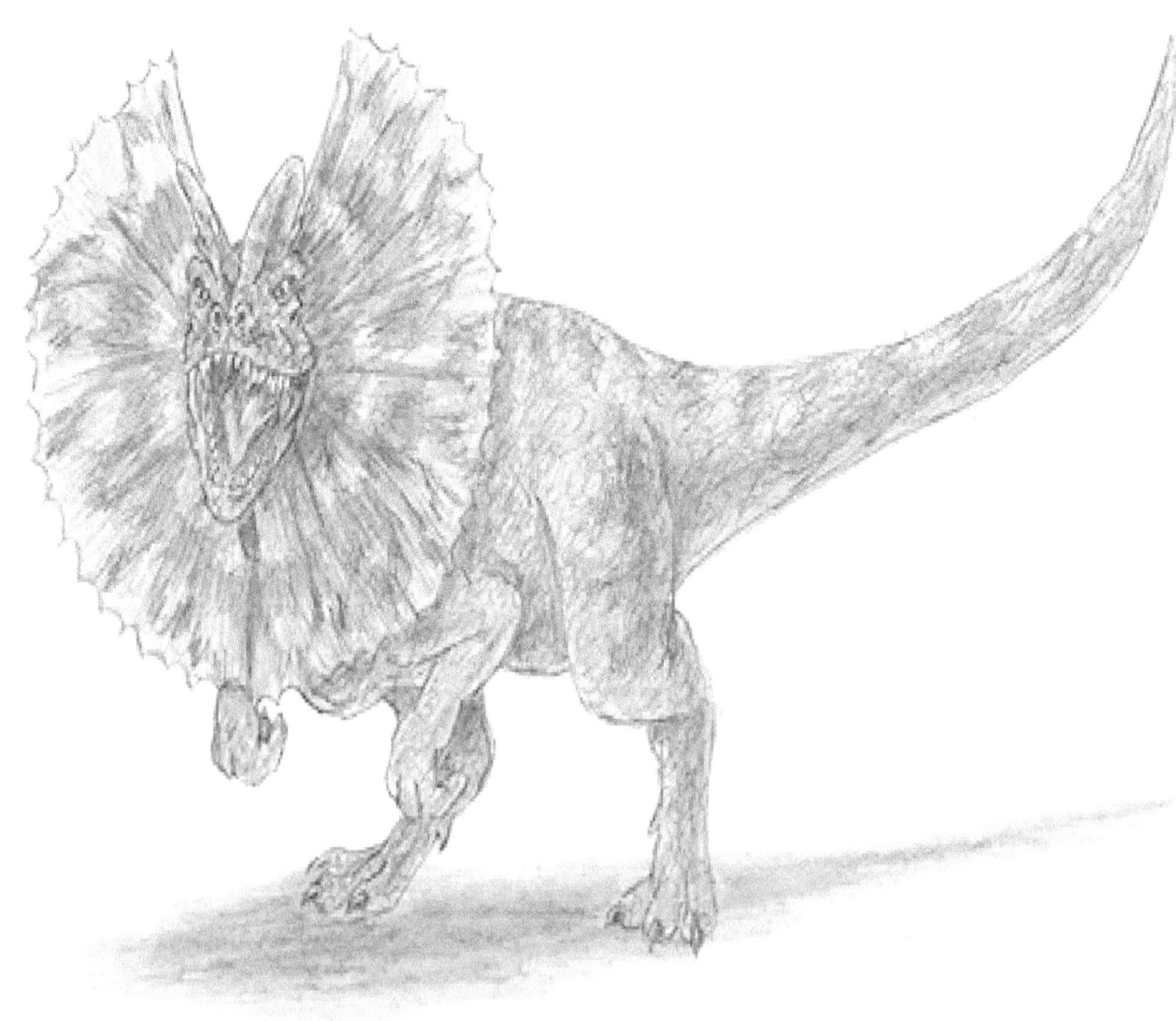

How to Draw a Styracosaurus

Step 1:

Draw a circle on the left side of the paper as a guide for the Styracosaurus' head. First make four small marks to indicate the circle's height and width. Then connect the marks using curved lines. If you're having a hard time drawing the circle, trace the outer rim of a coin, a lid or any other object with a circular edge.

Step 2:

Under the head, draw a curved line as a guide for the muzzle. The shape of the muzzle should be similar to the letter U. Pay attention to its size in relation to the dinosaur's head.

Step 3:

Make a mark high above the head to determine the height of the Styracosaurus' frill. Add another small mark on the right side of the head too. Now draw a sloping line on the left side of the head for the front part of the frill. To finish the guide for the frill, draw a line that curves around the top part of the head and ends at the mark on the right side.

Step 4:

At the top of the frill, draw four lines as guides for the frill spikes. The lines should start near the middle and curve outward. The spikes on the sides will be shorter, so make those guides smaller. Close to where the head meets the muzzle, on the left side, draw another curved line as a guide for the Styracosaurus' nose horn.

Step 5:

To the right of the head, draw a big circle as a guide for the front part of the body. Draw this circle like the head: make some marks, then connect the marks using curved lines. Notice the size of this circle in relation to the dinosaur's head.

Step 6:

On the right side, draw another circle as a guide for the back portion of the Styracosaurus' body. Draw this circle the same way and make it slightly smaller than the circle for the front part of the body.

Step 7:

Under the circle on the left, draw two angled lines as guides for the Styracosaurus dinosaur's front legs. Bend the lines to indicate where the joints will be. The foot on the left will be stepping forward, so draw that guide line sloping.

Step 8:

Draw two more angled lines under the circle on the right as guides for the hind legs. Pay attention to how these lines bend, as this will help you draw the Styracosaurus' joints and feet later on.

Step 9:

Draw two short, curved lines that connect the head to the body to create the neck. Draw two longer curved lines that connect the two big circles to finish the guidefor the body. On the right side of the body, draw two long, wavy lines as guides for the dinosaur's tail. The left side of the tail should be wide, and the right side should end at a thin, pointy tip.That's it for the guides! From this point on, press harder with your pencil for a more defined drawing.

Step 10:

Inside the head, near the middle, lightly sketch a small circle for the dinosaur's eye. When you get the placement and shape right, darken the lines. Make the top and bottom pointier. In the middle of the eye, draw a dot for the pupil. Off to the side, draw a tiny circle to represent glare. Draw a couple of curved lines above and below the eye for the eyelids. Add more curved lines around the eye for the skin's wrinkles. To the left of the eye, draw a curved line with small, triangle-like shapes on top for the Styracosaurus' spiky brow.

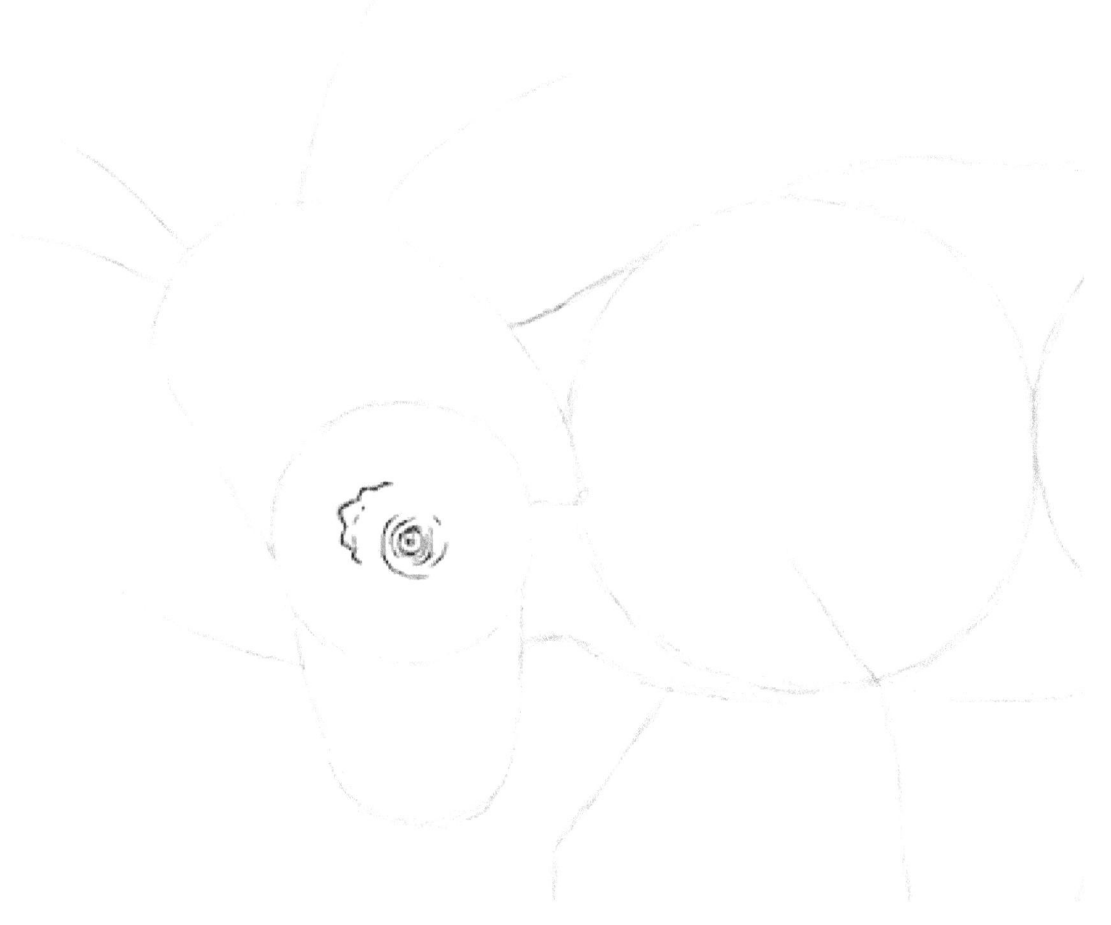

Step 11:

Use the line on the muzzle as a guide for drawing the horn on the nose. Follow the basic path of the guide and draw the shape of the horn around it. The shape of the horn should be wide at the base, get gradually thinner and end at a pointy tip. Add a few lines below the base of the Styracosaurus' horn for the wrinkles on the skin.

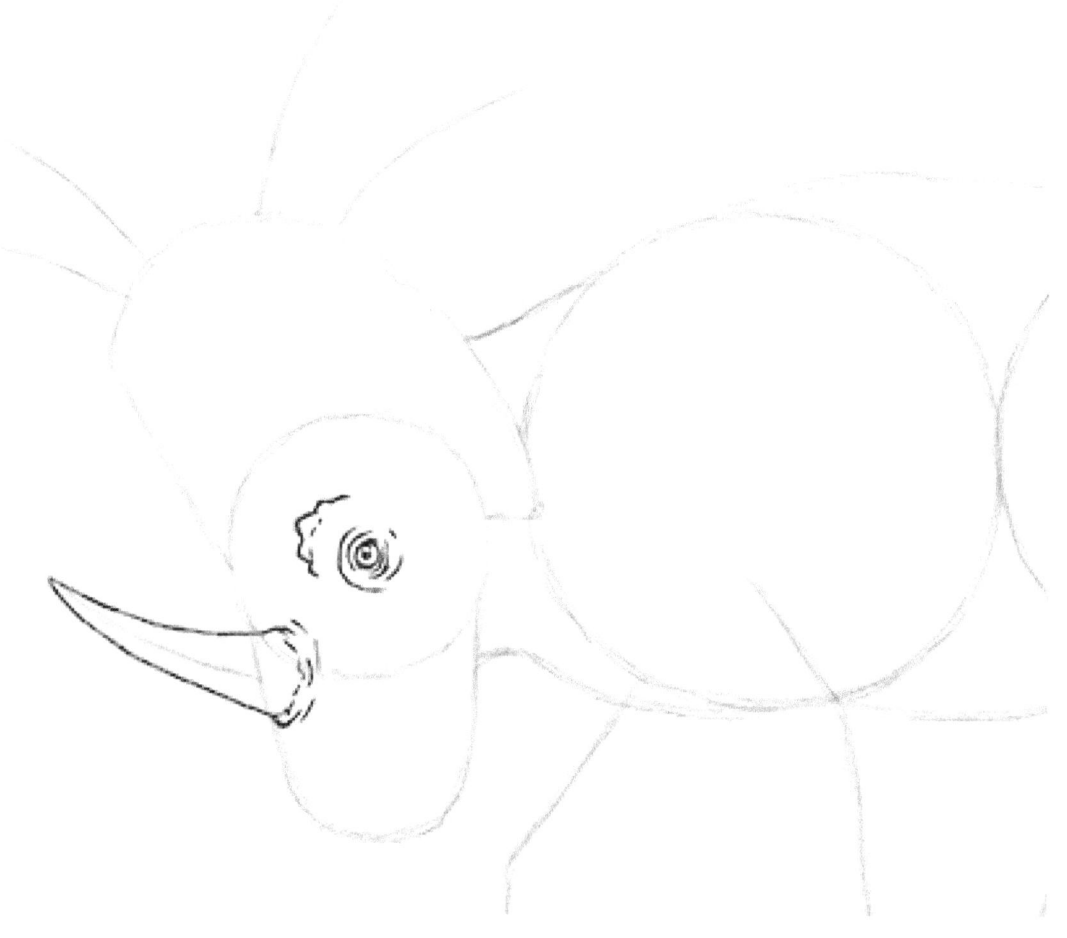

Step 12:

Use the U-shaped line under the head as a guide to draw the top part of the Styracosaurus' mouth. The mouth is shaped like a bird's beak, so make the top part curved and the tip pointy. Add a wavy line above the beak for the fleshy base of the mouth.

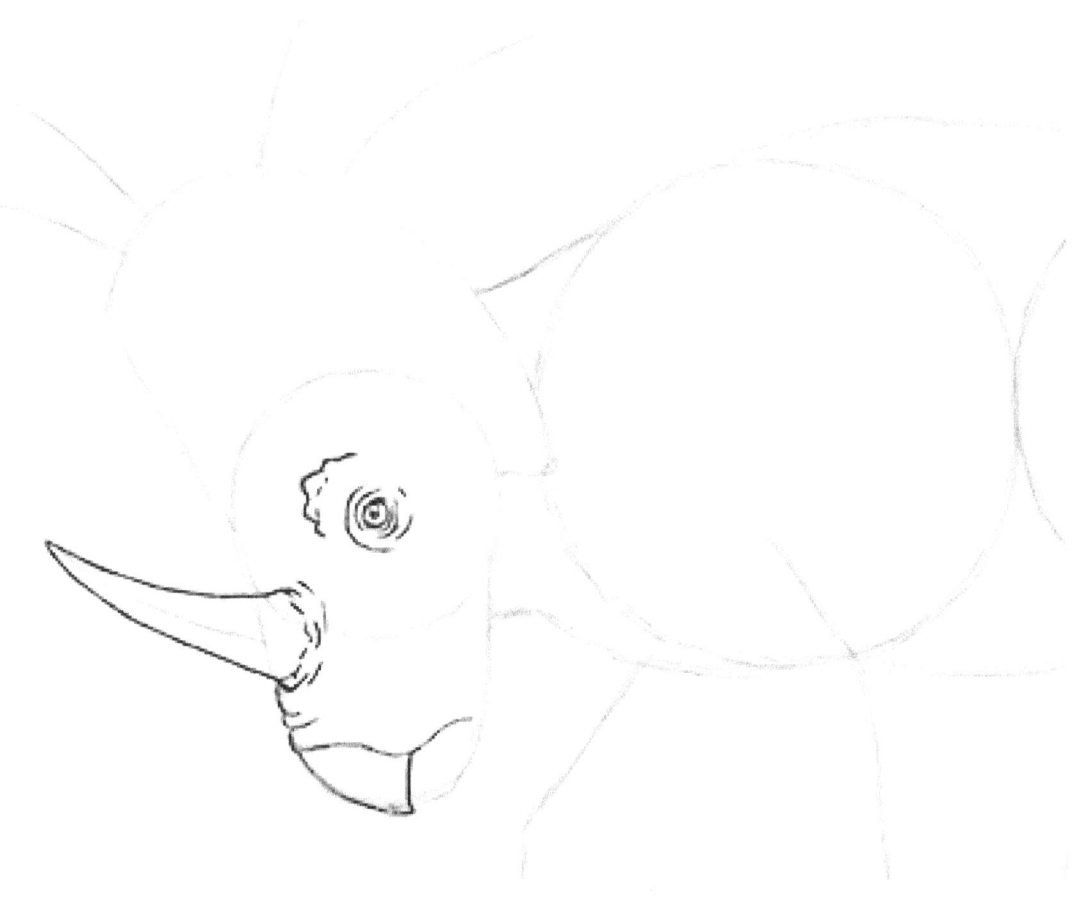

Step 13:

Draw the bottom part of the beak to the right and use the U-shaped line as a guide. Darken the right edge of the U- shaped guide to create the dinosaur's jaw. For the nostril, draw a slit shape on the edge of the initial circle guide.

Step 14:

Draw a series of triangle- like shapes along the left edge of the initial circle for the other brow. On the right side of the head, draw a larger triangle- like shape for the spike on the cheekbone. Draw a smaller triangle-like shape on the left side for the Styracosaurus' other cheekbone spike.

Step 15:

Use the lines on the frill as guides to draw the Styracosaurus' frill spikes. Just like with the nose horn, follow the path of the guide as you draw the shape of the spike around it. The base of the spikes should be wide, and the tops should end in pointy tips. Curve the shapes of the spikes outward. The spikes on the left will overlap each other a bit. You can also make the dinosaur's spikes a bit longer or shorter if you'd like.

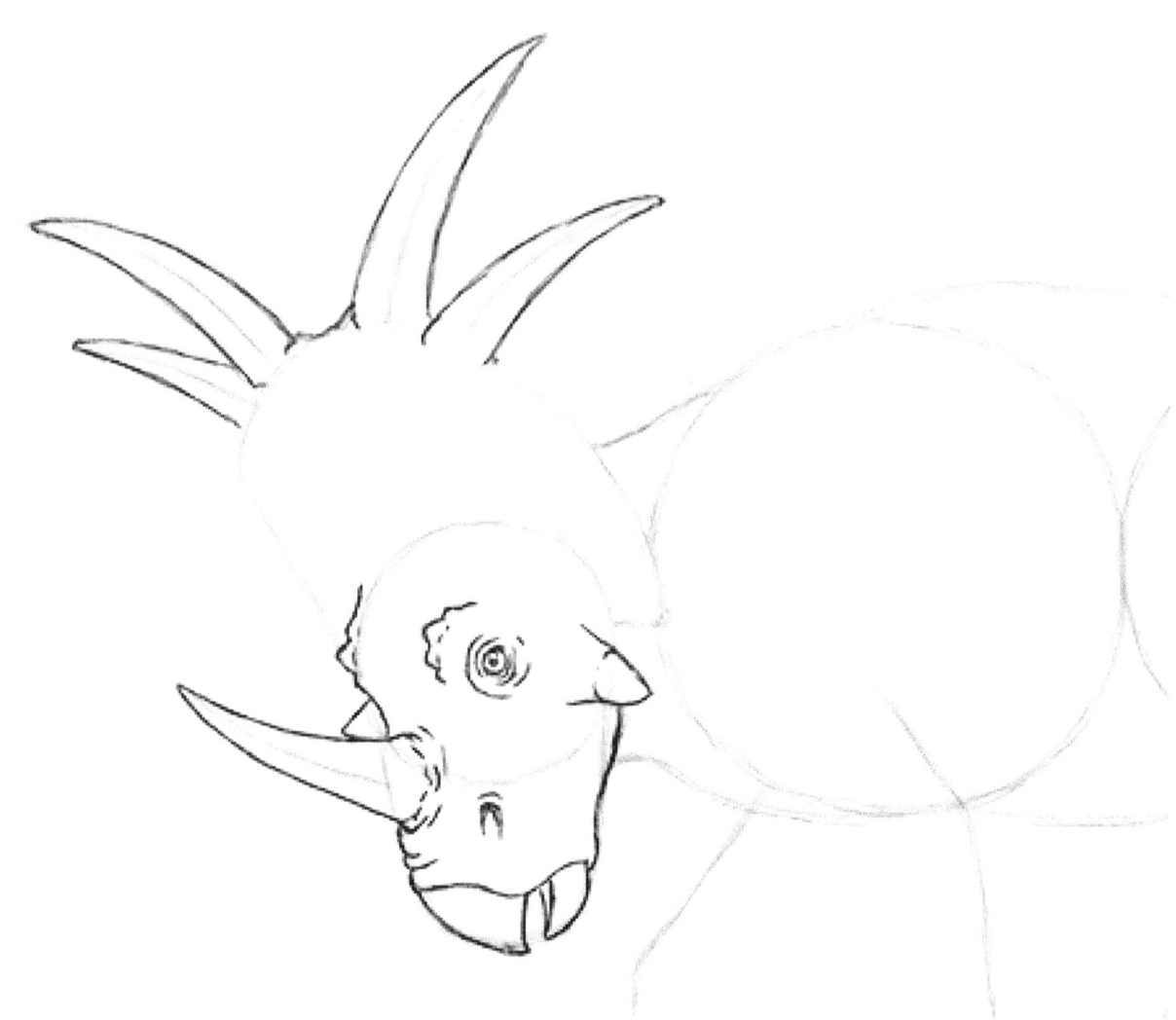

Step 16:

Continue adding more spikes along the edge of the frill guide. If you're having a hard time drawing the spikes freehand, draw a few guide lines first. Make the spikes smaller the farther down the frill they are.

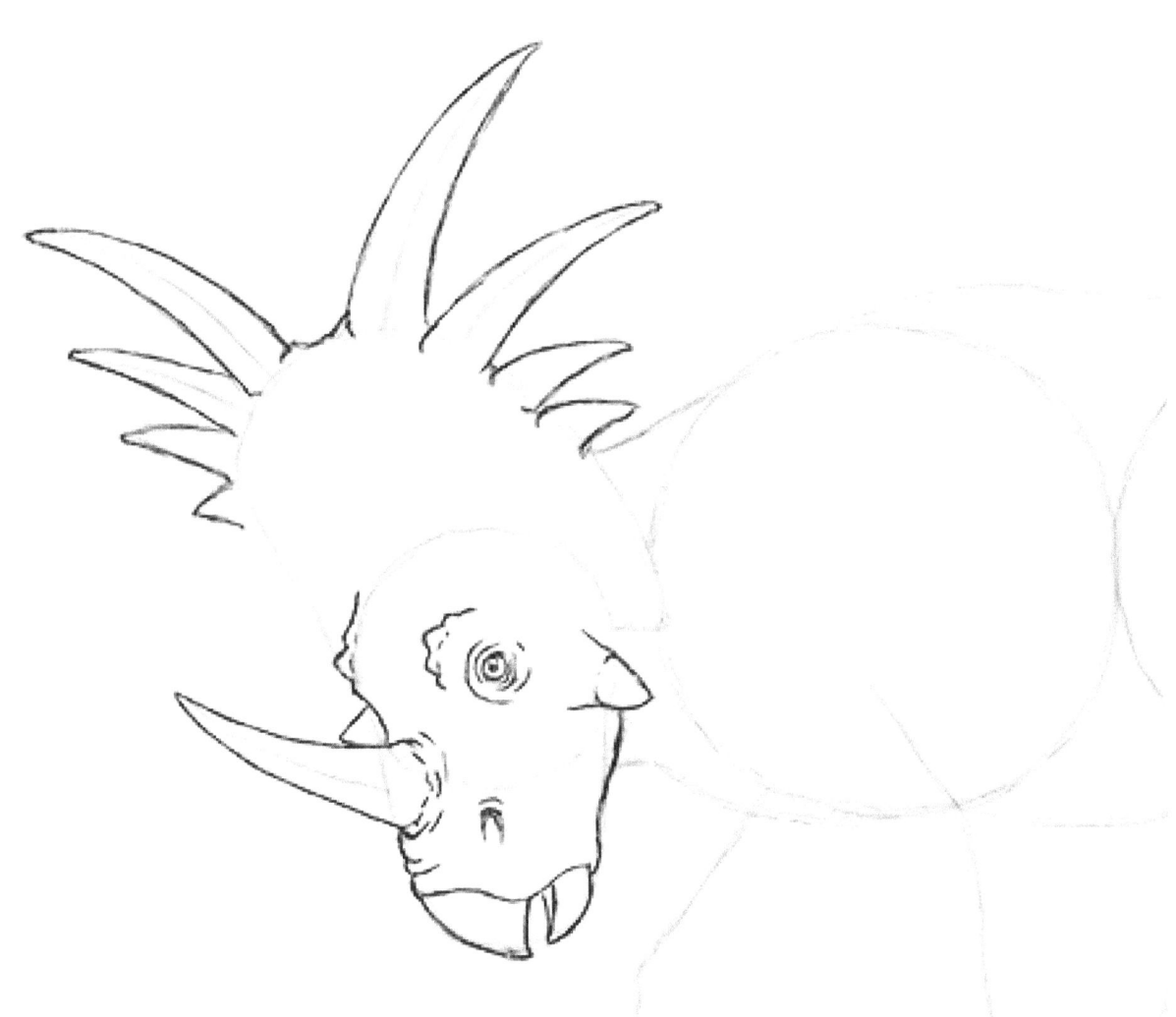

Step 17:

Keep drawing smaller spikes along the edges of the frill guide. These spikes should be similar to small triangles. The side of the frill should come in toward the eye a bit. Add a few curved, broken lines inside the frill to emphasize the rough texture. Add a couple of tiny triangle- shaped spikes at the top of the Styracosaurus' frill.

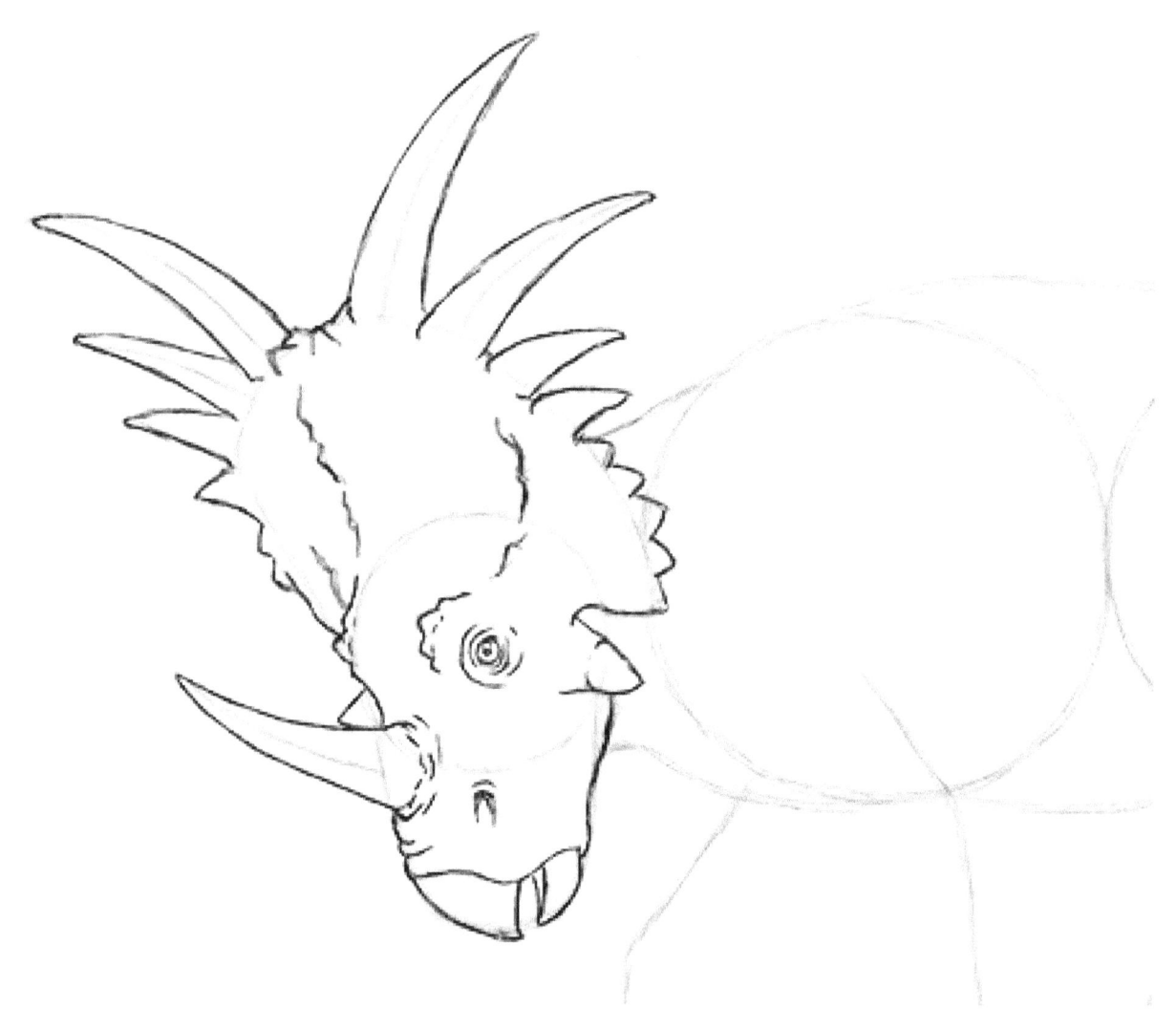

Step 18:

Use the second line from the left as a guide to draw the Styracosaurus' first front leg. Follow the path of the guide and lightly sketch the shape of the leg around it. When you get the shape and size of the leg right, darken the lines. Add a few extra lines at the joints for the folds on the skin. Draw a series of small triangle- like shapes at the bottom for the toes and hoof-like nails. The bottom of the foot should be wide and flat. The dinosaur's toes should be short and stubby. Use curved lines to draw the shape of the leg to emphasize the muscle structure. Add a few more lines within the shape for more folds on the skin.

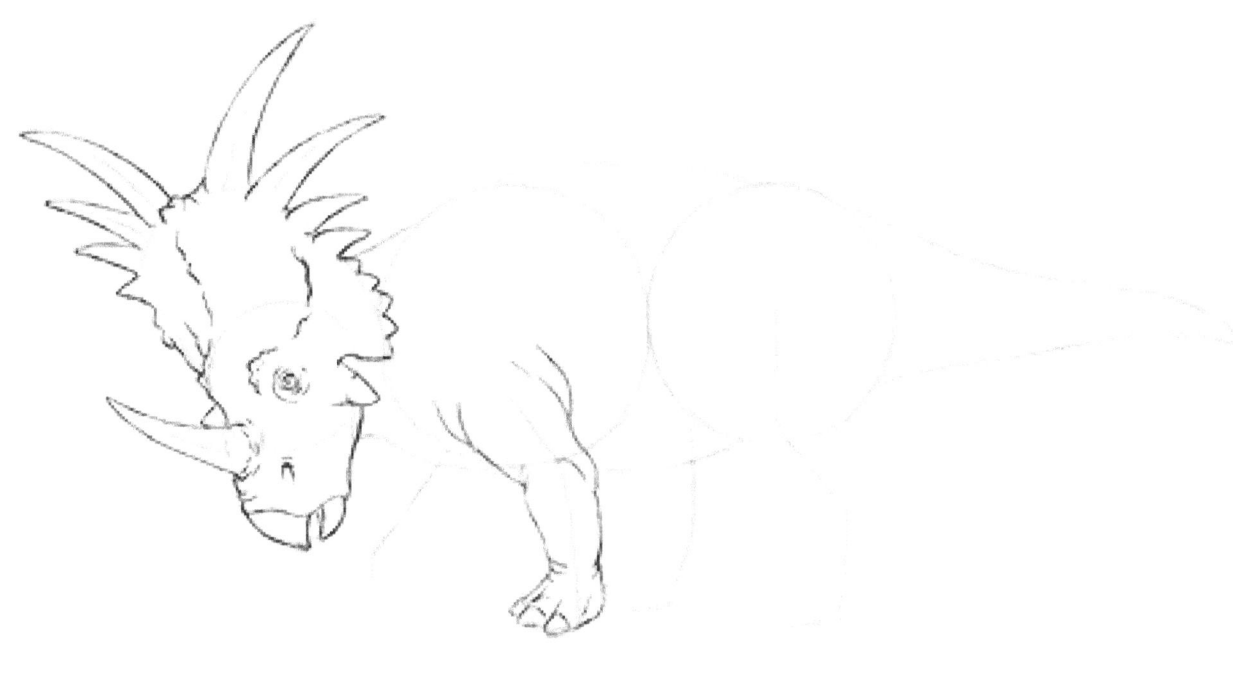

Step 19:

Use the sloping line on the left side as a guide to draw the other front leg the same way. Follow the path of the guide and draw the shape of the leg around it. Curve the shape of the leg so that it's raised and stepping forward. Because the Styracosaurus' leg is raised, the row of hoof-like nails will be at the bottom. Add curved lines along the way at the joints for the skin's wrinkles.

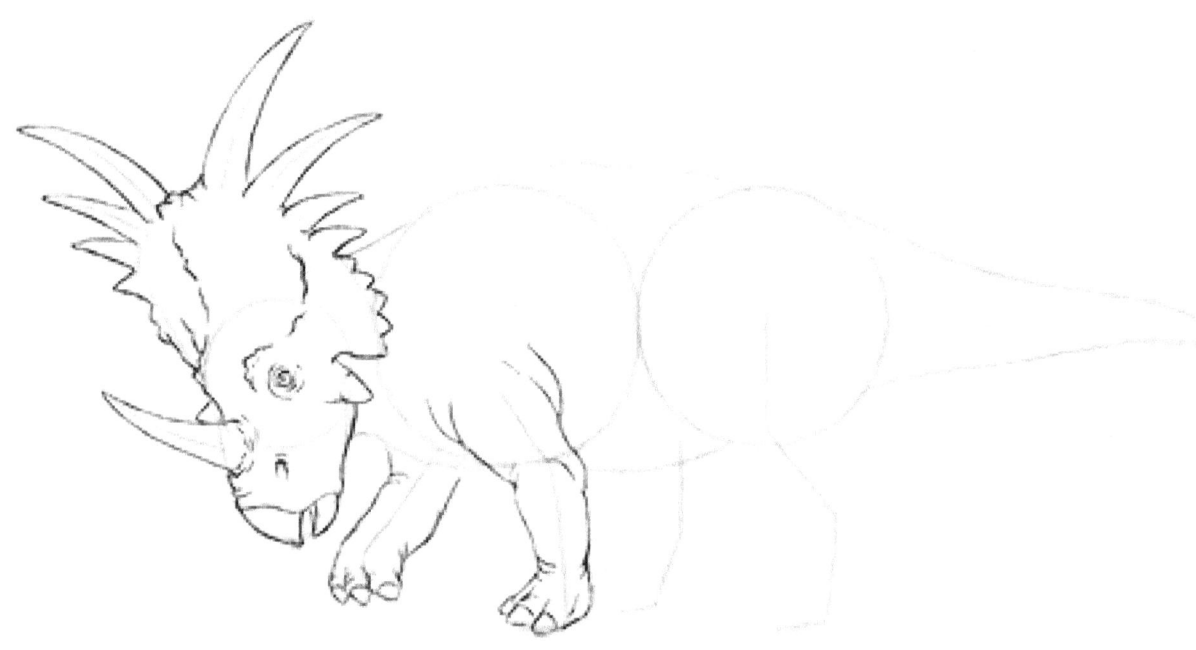

Step 20:

Use the line on the far right side as a guide to draw the hind leg that's on this side of the body. Follow the basic path of the guide and lightly sketch the shape of the leg around it. When you get the shape of the leg right, darken the lines. The top of the leg starts high inside the body. The top should also be pretty wide. Add the dinosaur's visible toes and hoof-like nails at the bottom. The bottom of the leg should be thinner than the top. Curve the lines to emphasize the muscle structure. Add wrinkles at the joints.

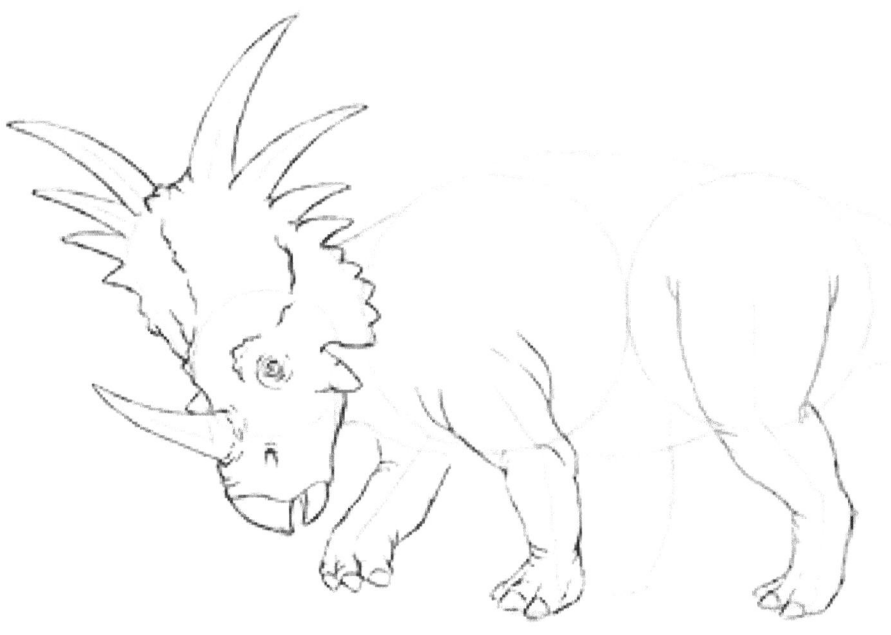

Step 21:

Use the last line under the dinosaur's body as a guide to draw the other hind leg the same way. Draw the shape of the leg around the guide and add the hoof-like nails at the bottom. The top of the leg will be hidden by the body, so only draw the lower, visible portion.

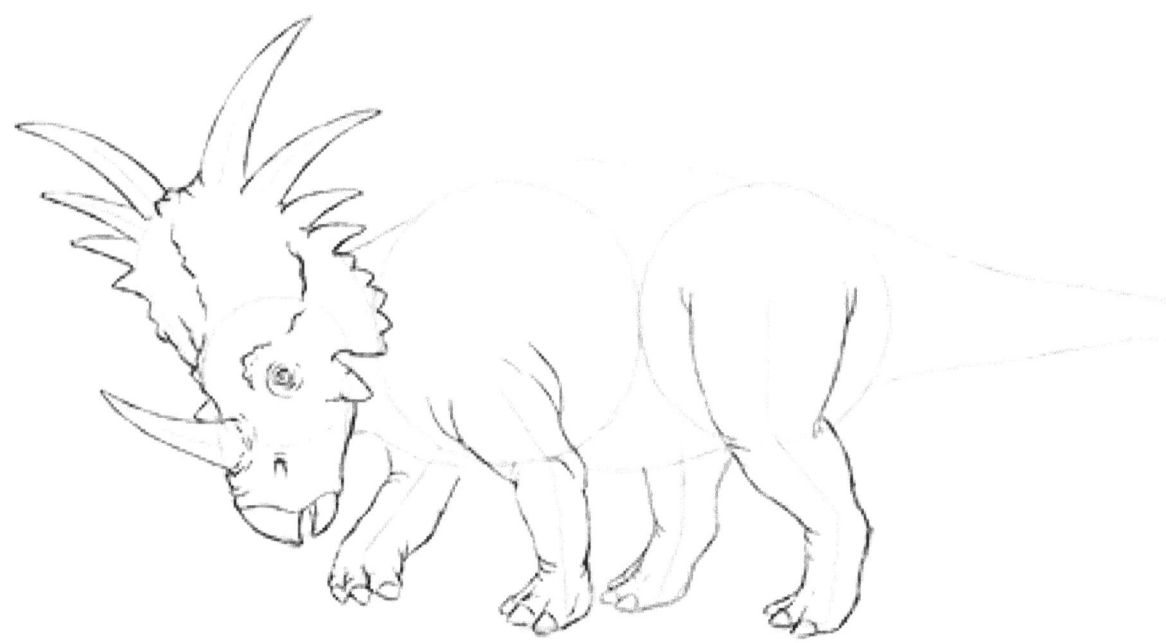

Step 22:

Use the remaining lines as guides to draw the rest of the Styracosaurus dinosaur's body. Simply darken the outer edges of the initial guide lines to create the shape of the body. Don't overlap the legs that are on this side of the body. Make the tail a bit wavier to make it less rigid and more organic.

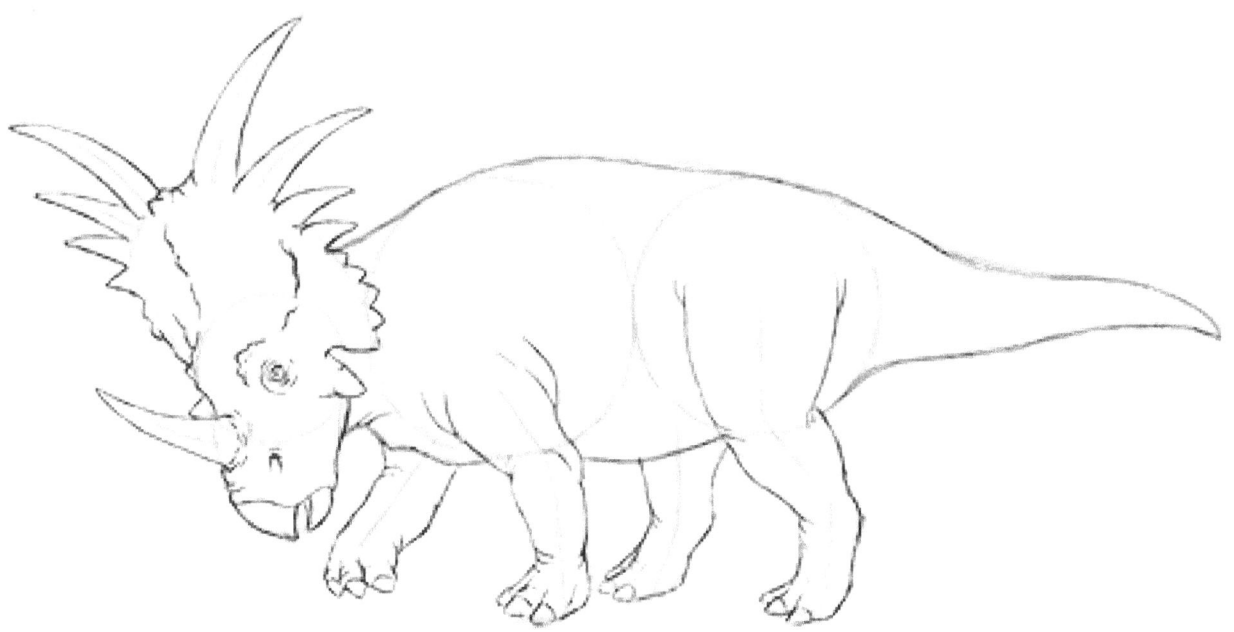

Step 23:

For a cleaner look, erase as much as you can of the initial guide lines. Don't worry about erasing all of the guides. It's okay to leave some behind. Re-draw any final sketch lines you may have accidentally erased.

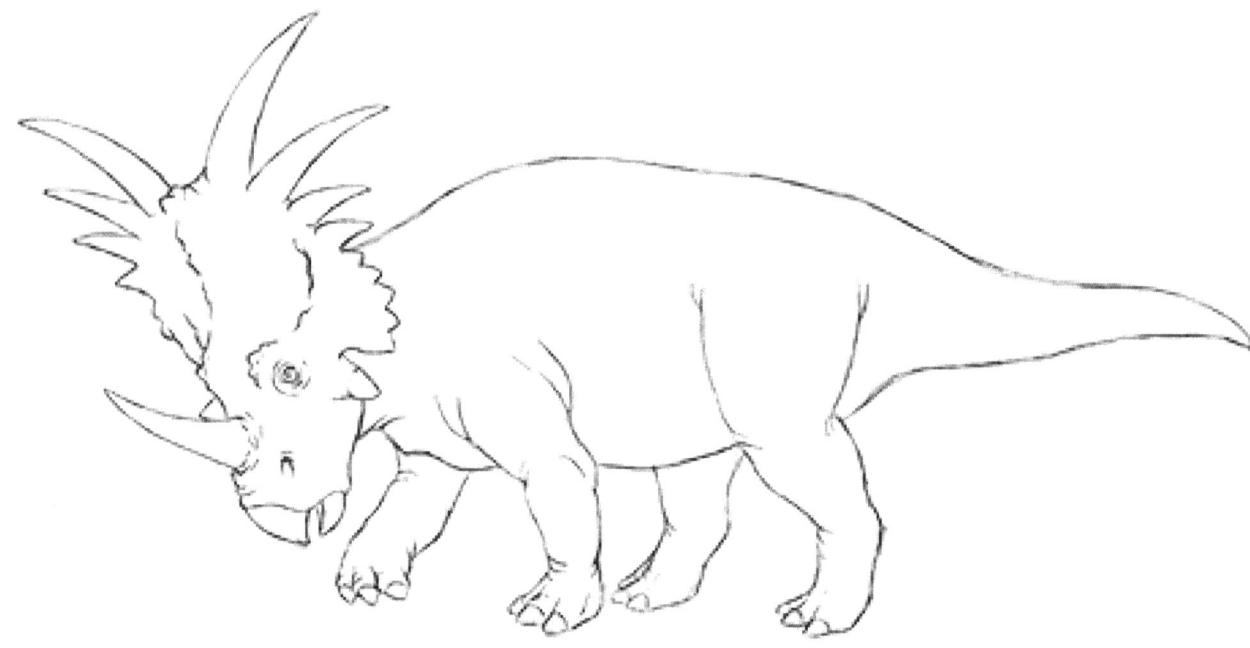

Final Step:

Add some shading to your Styracosaurus dinosaur drawing to give it more dimension and volume. Pick the direction of the light source when shading so that the shadows are consistent with it. Vary the pressure on your pencil to get different degrees of tonal value. Add the value lightly at first, then gradually build up to the level of darkness that you want.

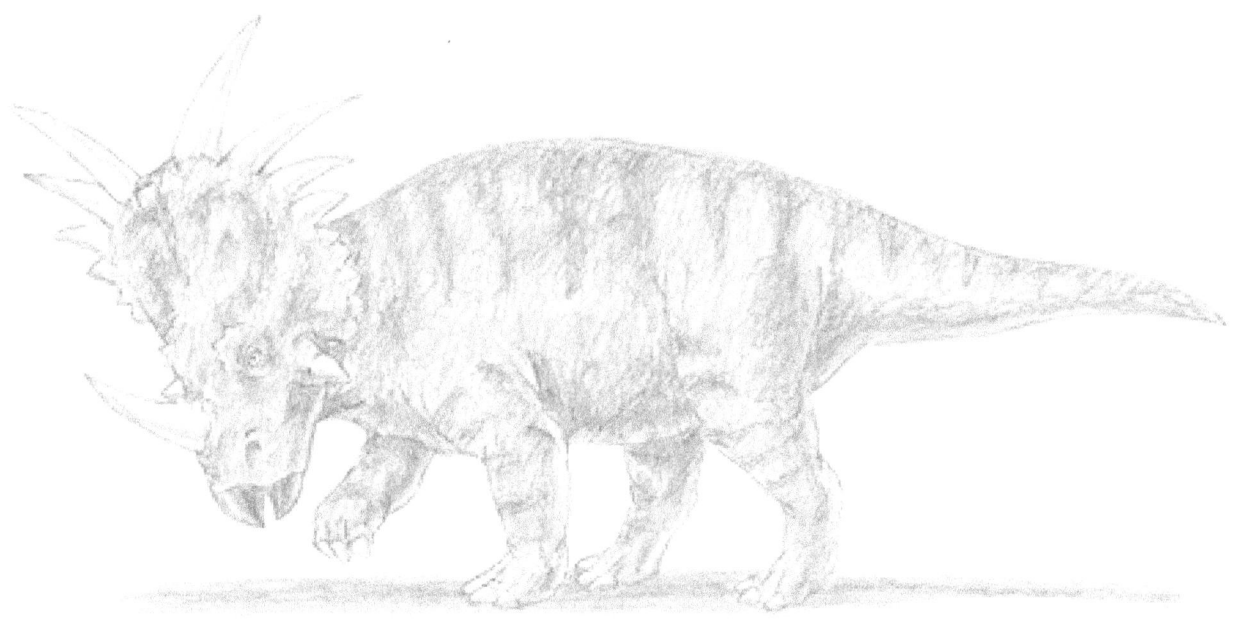